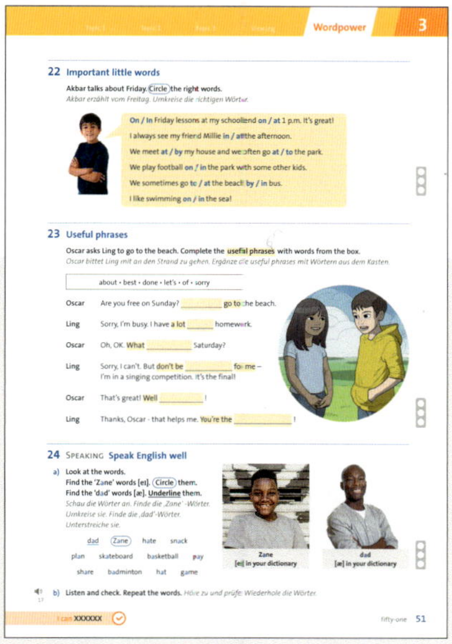

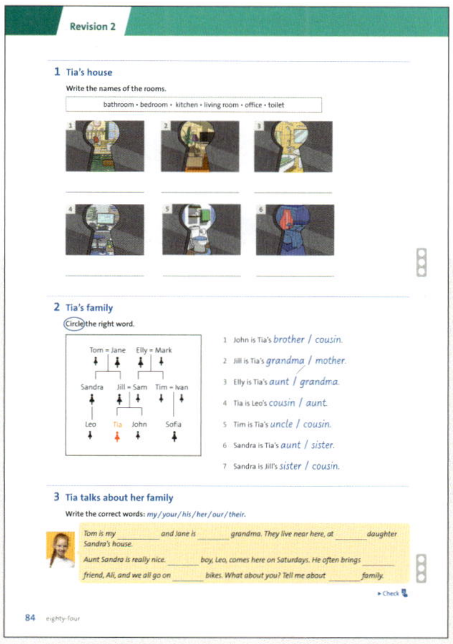


### *Wordpower*

Auf diesen Seiten findest du Übungen zu den Vokabeln der jeweiligen Units und kannst dein gesprochenes Englisch verbessern.

### *My learner log*

Hier kannst du auf die Unit zurückblicken und deinen Lernstand festhalten.

### *Revision*

Halte auf diesen Seiten inne und wiederhole, was du in den vorherigen Units gelernt hast.

## Dein Buch findest du auch in der Cornelsen Lernen App

Siehst du eines dieser Symbole in deinem Workbook, kannst du in deiner App ...

| Erklär-film | ▸ Digital help | ▸ Check |
|---|---|---|
| alle Hörtexte und Videos zu deinem Buch aufrufen. | auf Ideen und Hilfen zugreifen. | deine Antworten eigenständig überprüfen. |

# lighthouse 1

Workbook

*Im Auftrag des Verlages erarbeitet von*
Gwen Berwick, York
Sydney Thorne, York

*In Zusammenarbeit mit der Englischredaktion*
Klaus Unger (Projektleitung),
Karin Wedepohl (verantwortliche Redakteurin), Lisa Ahmadi, Doreen Arnold, Natalie-Monique Bernau, Bernd Freiling, Cornelia Frisse, Mara Leibowitz, Christine Maxwell, Jutta Seuren, Kathrin Spiegelberg, Silvia Wiedemann, Olivia Wintgens, Anja Zieschang

*Beratende Mitwirkung*
Sabine Bay, Cloppenburg; Ulrike Plänker, Sprockhövel

*Lizenzmanagement*
Silke Kirchhoff

*Illustrationen*
Harald Ardeias, Schelklingen; Irina Zinner, Hamburg

*Fotos*
Anja Poehlmann, Brighton

Für die freundliche Unterstützung danken wir der *Varndean School, Brighton*

*Umschlaggestaltung*
Rosendahl, Berlin

*Layoutkonzept*
Klein & Halm, Berlin

*Layout und technische Umsetzung*
Straive

Passend zum Workbook:
Sprechen, Aussprache, Wortschatz und Grammatik digital üben mit der mobilen App ChatClass. Erhältlich auch als PrintPlus-Klassenlizenz bei Nutzung des Arbeitsheftes.

**www.cornelsen.de**



Druck: Athesiadruck GmbH

1. Auflage, 1. Druck 2023
Workbook 1
ISBN 978-3-0603-5775-8

1. Auflage, 1. Druck 2023
Workbook 1 Lehrkräftefassung
ISBN 978-3-0603-5777-2

PEFC
PEFC/18-31-166
PEFC-zertifiziert
Dieses Produkt stammt aus nachhaltig bewirtschafteten Wäldern
www.pefc.de

# lighthouse 1

## Workbook

**Audios** online verfügbar unter
www.cornelsen.de/webcodes **Code:** muboki

Dein Workbook findest du auch in der Cornelsen Lernen App.
Siehst du eines dieser Symbole in deinem Workbook, findest du in der App …

- alle **Audios**
- alle **Videos** und **Erklärfilme**
- **Hilfen** und **Lösungen** zu ausgewählten Aufgaben

Cornelsen

**Titelbild**
Cornelsen/Personen: Anja Poehlmann, Brighton Pier: mauritius images/Steve Vidler

**Illustrationen**
**Cornelsen/Harald Ardeias**: S. 8, S. 10 1–3+5; S. 13 un.; S. 14 ob.li.+un.; S. 15 un.; S. 16 alle; S. 17 mi.; S. 18 alle; S. 20 ob.; S. 27 un.re.; S. 28 un.re.; S. 30–31; S. 33–34+37; S. 41 1–8; S. 42 ob.re.; S. 44 mi.; S. 45 1–8, S. 47 A–F; S. 50 1–6; S. 51 mi.re.; S. 53 alle außer Herz; S. 55 mi.; S. 59 1–6, S. 60 mi.; S. 61 un.; S. 65 un.re.; S. 74 mi.li.; S. 77 A–F; S. 83 ob.; S. 84 1–6; **Cornelsen/Irina Zinner:** S. 5 Möwe; S. 6 Möwen; S. 7 Möwe; S. 24–25 Möwen; S. 27 Möwe; S. 29 Möwe; S. 42 Möwe; S. 45 Möwe. S. 52; S. 56 Möwe; S. 59 Möwe, S. 68 Möwe; S. 78 Möwe; S. 81–82 Möwen; S. 88 Möwen; **Cornelsen/Raimo Bergt:** S. 10: 4; **Ungermeyer, Berlin:** S. 6 Pfeile; S. 7 Pfeile.

**Abbildungen**
**Umschlaginnenseite vorne (U2):** Siehe S. 12, 13, 49; **S. 1** Siehe S. 24, 51, 84; **S. 3** un.li.: Cornelsen/Inhouse/Anne Weingarten; **S. 5** li.: Cornelsen/Anja Poehlmann; **S. 7** Hintergrund: Shutterstock.com/vetryanaya_o, Pfeile: **S. 9** 1: Shutterstock.com/Utekhina Anna, 2: Shutterstock.com/Four Oaks, 3: Shutterstock.com/PHOTOCREO Michal Bednarek, 4: Shutterstock.com/Eric Isselee, 5: Shutterstock.com/bluedog studio, 6: stock.adobe.com/Arija, 7: Shutterstock.com/SmileKorn, 8: Shutterstock.com/Eric Isselee, Emoticons: stock.adobe.com/streptococcus, mi.li.: Shutterstock.com/ANURAK PONGPATIMET; **S. 10** A: Shutterstock.com/New Africa, B: Shutterstock.com/hurricanehank, C: Shutterstock.com/panyajampatong, D: Shutterstock.com/Roman Samborskyi, E: Shutterstock.com/Rudenko Alla, F: Shutterstock.com/Ekaterina Zateeva; **S. 11** mi.: stock.adobe.com/sepy, mi.li.: stock.adobe.com/mma23, mi.re.: stock.adobe.com/anamejia18, Flaggen: stock.adobe.com/Porcupen; **S. 12** B: stock.adobe.com/pololia, C: stock.adobe.com/Jacek Chabraszewski, D: stock.adobe.com/DragonImages, E: stock.adobe.com/Alena Yakusheva, F: ClipDealer GmbH/Wavebreak Media LTD, G: stock.adobe.com/yurakrasil, H: stock.adobe.com/JackF, mi.: Cornelsen/Anja Poehlmann; **S. 15** ob.re.: stock.adobe.com/Syda Productions/lev dolgachov, A: Shutterstock.com/F8 studio, B: Shutterstock.com/Tyler Olson; **S. 19** A: stock.adobe.com/.shock, B: Images, C: stock.adobe.com/vladimirnenezic, D: mauritius images/Johnér, E: Cornelsen/Anja Poehlmann, F: stock.adobe.com/Gudellaphoto; **S. 20** 1: stock.adobe.com/Imcsike, 2: stock.adobe.com/Fabio Principe, 3: stock.adobe.com/SB Arts Media, 4: stock.adobe.com/Photographee.eu/Katarzyna Bialasiewicz, 5: Shutterstock.com/spacezerocom, 6: stock.adobe.com/Africa Studio; **S. 23** un.re.: Cornelsen/Oliver Meibert; **S. 25** mi.: Cornelsen/Anja Poehlmann; **S. 26** Dad's dad: Shutterstock.com/Alejandro Camacho B, Dad's mum: Shutterstock.com/PHILIPIMAGE, Mum's mum: Shutterstock.com/Caftor, My dad: Shutterstock.com/Joshua Rainey Photography, My mum: stock.adobe.com/francescoridolfi.com/Rido, Jane: stock.adobe.com/#CNF, Mike: stock.adobe.com/goodluz, Olivia: Shutterstock.com/Erika Cross, Oscar: stock.adobe.com/Peredniankina, Freddie: Shutterstock.com/Max Topchii, Amelia: Shutterstock.com/Olga Sapegina; **S. 27** cats: Shutterstock.com/Peti74, hamsters: mauritius images/alamy stock photo/Maximilian Weinzierl, dogs: Shutterstock.com/thka, horses: Shutterstock.com/Kwadrat, fish: Shutterstock.com/panpilai paipa, parrots: Shutterstock.com/Super Prin, snakes: Shutterstock.com/Mufti Adi Utomo, rabbits: Shutterstock.com/Kolomiyets Viktoriya; **S. 29** mi.li.: Shutterstock.com/BearFotos, mi.re.: Shutterstock.com/anggitirta, un.li.: Shutterstock.com/Felipe Cespedes G, un.re.: Shutterstock.com/Alex Milan; **S. 32** 1+3: Shutterstock.com/Africa Studio, 2: Shutterstock.com/Evgeny Karandaev, 4: Shutterstock.com/donatas1205, 5: Imago Stock & People GmbH/Shotshop, 6: Shutterstock.com/Mile Atanasov, 7: Shutterstock.com/YK; **S. 40** ob.li.: stock.adobe.com/Peredniankina, A: mauritius images/alamy stock photo/Katy Blackwood, B: stock.adobe.com/VaLiza/valiza14, C: mauritius images/alamy stock photo/John Michaels, D: Shutterstock.com/Kryvenok Anastasiia, E: stock.adobe.com/Suriyo; **S. 41** deutsche Flagge: www.coulorbox.de, britische Flagge: Shutterstock.com/Jeerasak banditram; **S. 43** re.: Shutterstock.com/ANURAK PONGPATIMET; **S. 45** ob.: Shutterstock.com/valeryvoronessa; **S. 46** ob.: Shutterstock.com/Varlamova Lydmila; **S. 48** Anna: Shutterstock.com/ShotPrime Studio, Max: Shutterstock.com/Rohappy, mi.re.: Cornelsen/Oliver Meibert; **S. 49** mi.re.: Cornelsen/Grasshopper Films; **S. 51** ob.re.: Shutterstock.com/Rohit Seth, un.mi.: Cornelsen/Anja Poehlmann, un.re.: Shutterstock.com/Daniel M Ernst; **S. 53** Herz: Shutterstock.com/pking4th; **S. 54** mi.li.: Shutterstock.com/BearFotos, mi.: Zurijeta, mi.re.: Shutterstock.com/Lisa F. Young; **S. 56** A: Imago Stock & People GmbH/Loop Images/Chris Harris, B: Imago Stock & People GmbH/Tim Oram, C: stock.adobe.com/Kevin Eaves, D: Imago Stock & People GmbH/robertharding/Baxter Bradford, E: stock.adobe.com/Nomad_Soul, F: stock.adobe.com/lev dolgachov/Syda Productions, G: Imago Stock & People GmbH/robertharding/Frank Fell, un.re.: mauritius images/alamy stock photo/keith morris; **S. 58** deutsche Flagge: www.coulorbox.de, britische Flagge: Shutterstock.com/Jeerasak banditram, un.re.: Cornelsen/Anja Poehlmann; **S. 60** un.li.: mauritius images/Westend61, un.re.: stock.adobe.com/Peredniankina; **S. 62** ob.li.: Imago Stock & People GmbH/robertharding/Stuart Black, ob.re.+un.re.: stock.adobe.com/cyclingscot, un.li.: Imago Stock & People GmbH/robertharding/Jeanne Rawlings; **S. 63** ob.li.: Shutterstock.com/Zelimir Zarkovic, ob.re.: stock.adobe.com/lesniewski, mi.re.: mauritius images/alamy stock photo/Howard Taylor; **S. 64** ob.li.: mauritius images/alamy stock photo/Jason Chillmaid, ob.re.: mauritius images/alamy stock photo/Hoi Tung Wong, mi.re.: Shutterstock.com/Greenni; **S. 70** A: Shutterstock.com/Alexander Raths, B: Shutterstock.com/azure1, C: Shutterstock.com/Geshas, D: Shutterstock.com/AtlasStudio, E: Shutterstock.com/nortongo, F: Shutterstock.com/Valery121283, G: Shutterstock.com/AnVdErGiA, H: Shutterstock.com/morgenstjerne, I: Shutterstock.com/Valentyn Volkov, J: Shutterstock.com/MaraZe; **S. 71** mi.: Shutterstock.com/Brigida Soriano; **S. 72** A: stock.adobe.com/karelnoppe, B: Shutterstock.com/aldegonde, C: Shutterstock.com/Ixepop, D: Shutterstock.com/Apollofoto, E: Shutterstock.com/RedPanda21, F: stock.adobe.com/patramansky; **S. 73** 1: Shutterstock.com/Vitalinka, 2: Shutterstock.com/aarrows, 3+4: Shutterstock.com/Eladora, 5: Shutterstock.com/shaineast, 6: Shutterstock.com/majivecka; **S. 75** A: Shutterstock.com/Marietjie, B: stock.adobe.com/Serge Aubert, C: stock.adobe.com/Margarita, D: stock.adobe.com/hartphotography; **S. 76** A: Shutterstock.com/MaraZe, B: stock.adobe.com/tpzijl, C: Shutterstock.com/Pawel_Brzozowski, D: Shutterstock.com/Inked Pixels, E: Shutterstock.com/Joe Gough, F: Shutterstock.com/azure1, G: Shutterstock.com/Valentyn Volkov, H: Shutterstock.com/ivanoffotography; **S. 77** 1: Shutterstock.com/Perutskyi Petro, 2: Shutterstock.com/bigacis, 3: Shutterstock.com/Picture Partners, 4: Shutterstock.com/Andrii Horulko, 5: Shutterstock.com/Gita Kulinitch Studio, 6: Shutterstock.com/Maher Mhl; **S. 78** ob.li.: Shutterstock.com/sirtravelalot; **S. 79** mi.re.: Cornelsen/Grasshopper Films; **S. 80** un.re.: Shutterstock.com/Med_Ved; **S. 84** mi.li.: stock.adobe.com/ SENRYU, un.li.: Shutterstock.com/ViDI Studio; **S. 85** ob.re.: Shutterstock.com/ViDI Studio; **S. 86** ob.li.: Imago Stock & People GmbH/robertharding/Jeanne Rawlings, ob.re.+un.re.: stock.adobe.com/cyclingscot, un.li.: Imago Stock & People GmbH/robertharding/Stuart Black

## This quiz helps you get to know your *Lighthouse* student's book.

**Mit diesem Quiz lernst du dein *Lighthouse*-Schulbuch kennen.**
**Du kannst es allein oder mit einem Partner / einer Partnerin lösen.**

1 Wie viele Units hat dein *Lighthouse*-Schulbuch? ☐

2 Jede Unit beginnt mit einer Übersicht darüber, was du darin lernen wirst: *Nach dieser Unit kann ich …*

Was lernst du als erstes in Unit 2? Schaue auf S. 45 nach.

______________________________

______________________________

3 In Unit 1 auf den Seiten 18–19 lernst du die Lehrwerkskinder kennen. Nenne ihre Namen.

______________________________

4 Was bedeutet dieses Symbol? ☒

Schaue am Anfang des Schulbuchs auf den *So lernst du mit Lighthouse-Seiten* nach.

______________________________

5 In der *Cornelsen Lernen App* findest du viele nützliche Dinge. Welches Symbol im Buch weist auf digitale Hilfen hin?

Schaue am Anfang des Schulbuchs auf den *So lernst du mit Lighthouse-Seiten* nach.

🔊 ☐ ▶ ☐ 👆 ☐

6 Auf vielen Seiten findest du unten das Digital quiz -Symbol.

Was kannst du hier tun?

Schaue am Anfang des Schulbuchs auf den *So lernst du mit Lighthouse-Seiten* nach.

______________________________

______________________________

7 Was bedeuten diese 3 Begriffe in der *Diff bank*? Ordne die Buchstaben zu.

Schaue am Anfang des Schulbuchs auf den *So lernst du mit Lighthouse-Seiten* nach.

☐ More practice ☐ More help

☐ Parallel exercise

A einfachere Variante einer Übung
B Hilfen zu den Aufgaben
C weitere Übungen

8 Wie heißen die letzten 4 orangefarbenen Seiten jeder Unit, auf denen du dein Wissen überprüfen kannst?

______________________________

9 Im Language File (LF) kannst du Grammatikregeln nachschauen. Was wird im LF 3 auf S. 175 erklärt?

- ☐ Das Verb *be*
- ☐ Der Plural der Nomen
- ☐ Die Wortstellung

10 Im Skills file (SF) findest du Hinweise und Tipps, die dir beim Lernen helfen. Was lernst du im SF 3 auf S. 168?

- ☐ Wörter umschreiben
- ☐ Buchstabieren
- ☐ Einen Kurzvortrag halten

11 Am Ende des Buches findest du eine Karte der Britischen Inseln. In welcher Stadt wohnt die Möwe Scout?

B _ _ _ _ _ _ _

12 Im *Vocabulary* findest du die neuen Wörter aus jeder Unit. Lies den Eintrag zu *chocolate* auf S. 217. Worauf musst du achten?

______________________________

13 Auf S. 263 kannst nachschauen, wenn du eine Arbeitsanweisung nicht verstanden hast. Schau dort nach, was die Anweisung „*Take turns.*" bedeutet.

______________________________

14 Auf den *Let's talk*-Seiten findest du nützliche Redewendungen. Wozu dienen die Redewendungen unter Punkt 7 auf S. 200?

______________________________

**Prima! Nun weißt du schon viel über dein *Lighthouse*-Schulbuch.**
**Du kannst deine Lösungen in der App überprüfen.** Check

# Hello!
# Nice to meet you

## 1 Hello

► SB, p. 13

**Look at the picture. Write the words.**
*Schau das Bild an. Schreibe die Wörter.*

about • dog • football • ~~hello~~ • hungry • I'm • like • meet • name • see • what

I can introduce myself.

## 2 Animals

► SB, p. 14

**Find the animals: → ↓ ↘. Write the correct words.**
*Finde die Tiere: → ↓ ↘. Schreibe die richtigen Wörter auf.*

| | | | | | | | |
|---|---|---|---|---|---|---|---|
| E | J | P | I | X | R | A | D |
| N | L | I | O | N | U | P | V |
| H | R | E | T | M | H | N | D |
| Q | P | G | P | J | S | D | O |
| C | A | T | F | H | N | M | G |
| O | R | M | I | D | A | B | M |
| M | R | D | O | K | K | N | I |
| F | O | B | C | N | E | L | T |
| X | T | D | A | G | K | Y | Q |
| T | A | H | O | R | S | E | G |
| J | B | I | W | R | A | G | Y |

1 
d o g

2 
_ _ _ _ _ _ _ _

3 
_ _ _

4 
_ _ _ _ _ _

5 
_ _ _ _ _

6 
_ _ _ _ _

7 
_ _ _ _ _ _

8 
_ _ _ _

## 3 Hobbies

► SB, p. 15

**Read what Ling says. Then complete the smileys next to each picture.** *Lies was Ling sagt. Dann ergänze die Smileys neben jedem Bild.*

| | | |
|---|---|---|
| I love | I like | I don't like |

*I love listening to music and I like drawing. I don't like dancing.*

*I like taking photos, but I don't like swimming. I love football.*

1 

2 

3 

4 

5 

6 

I can talk about what I like.

## 4 Oscar's things

► SB, p. 15

**Look at the pictures. Write what Oscar says.**
*Schau dir die Bilder an. Schreibe auf, was Oscar sagt.*

| | | | |
|---|---|---|---|
| My | cap<br>rucksack<br>bike<br>football<br>phone | is | black.<br>blue.<br>green.<br>purple.<br>white.<br>grey. |

1 *My cap is green.*

2 ____________________

3 ____________________

4 __________ *and* __________

5 ____________________

1 

2 

3 

4 

5 

## 5 LISTENING My favourite hobby

01

► SB, p. 16

**Look at pictures A-F. Then listen to six kids and write the letter of their favourite hobbies (A-F).**
*Schau dir die Bilder A-F an. Dann höre sechs Kindern zu und schreibe den Buchstaben ihres Lieblingshobbys auf (A-F).*

A 

B 

C 

D 

E 

F 

1 Adil ____ 2 Lola ____ 3 Layla ____ 4 Connor ____ 5 Jack ____ 6 Anya ____

## 6 In class

► SB, p. 17

a) **Write the correct words.** *Schreibe die richtigen Wörter auf.*

books • down • hand • look • please • ~~up~~

1 *Stand* up ____________.

2 *Open your* ____________.

3 *Put your* ____________ *up.*

4 *Listen,* ____________.

5 *Sit* ____________.

6 ____________ *at the board.*

b) **Mime an instruction[1]. Your partner says it.** *Stelle eine Anweisung pantomimisch dar. Deine Partnerin / Dein Partner sagt sie auf Englisch.*

Partner A – 3 instructions
Partner B – 3 instructions

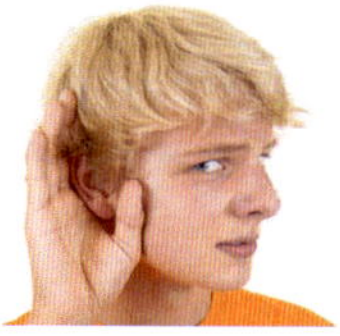

*Listen, please.*

*Yes, right!*

## 7 In your book

► SB, p. 17

**Match the English words**  **and the German words** .

*Ordne die englischen Wörter den deutschen zu.*

| | | | | |
|---|---|---|---|---|
| 1 | **Find** Scout. | D | A | Schreibe die richtigen Wörter. |
| 2 | **Complete** the song. | | B | Vervollständige das Lied. |
| 3 | Listen and **repeat**. | | C | Ordne die Wörter den Bildern zu. |
| 4 | **Write** the correct **words**. | | D | Finde Scout. |
| 5 | **Right** or **wrong**? | | E | Höre zu und wiederhole. |
| 6 | **Match** the words and the **pictures**. | | F | Richtig oder falsch? |

[1] **instruction** *Anweisung*

I can **understand classroom English.**

# Unit 1
# My new school

## 1 Sports and hobbies

▸ SB, p. 19

**Write the seven words from the box under the right pictures.**
*Schreibe die sieben Wörter aus dem Kästchen unter die richtigen Bilder.*

A

coding • cooking • dancing • parkour • swimming • walking • yoga

B

c ______________

C

w ______________

D

c ______________

E

p ______________

F

y ______________

G

s ______________

H

d ______________

## 2 Zane and you

▸ Digital help ▸ SB, p. 19

a) **Write the missing words.**
*Schreibe die fehlenden Wörter auf.*

about • from • I'm • is • years

1 Hi. __________ Zane. What's your name?

2 I'm eleven __________ old.
How old are you?

3 I'm __________ Brighton.
What about you?

4 I like cooking.
What __________ you?

5 My favourite sport __________ swimming.
And you?

b) **Now answer Zane's questions.**
*Nun beantworte Zanes Fragen.*

1 Hi. I'm ______________

2 I'm ______________

3 I'm ______________
______________

4 I like ______________
______________

5 My ______________
______________



I can understand students at a British school.

## 3 Lily, Zane, Sunita and Noah

▶ Digital help ▶ SB, p. 20

**Write the missing words.**
*Schreibe die fehlenden Wörter auf.*

class • happy • school • tired • uniform

| | | |
|---|---|---|
| 1 | sohocl | Lily, Zane, Sunita and Noah are all at ________________. |
| 2 | terid | Zane is busy and ________________. |
| 3 | hppay | Lily is ________________ about the school tie. |
| 4 | ufinrom | Sunita and Noah like the ________________. |
| 5 | csals | Sunita and Noah are in ________________ 7C. |

## 4 Language *a/an* In a safari park

▶ SB, p. 21

a) **Read the sentences in 4b). In the underlined words, highlight the first letter in red if it is a vowel (A, E, I, O, U) and in blue if it is a consonant.** *Lies die Sätze in 4b). Markiere den ersten Buchstaben der unterstrichenen Wörter in Rot, wenn es ein Vokal ist (A, E, I, O, U) und in Blau, wenn es ein Konsonant ist.*

b) **Now circle *a* or *an*.** *Umkreise nun a oder an.*

!
*an:* wenn das folgende Wort mit A, E, I, O, U beginnt

I can see (1) **a / an** animal. It's (2) **a / an** big animal. It's (3) **a / an** elephant. That's cool!

I can see (4) **a / an** animal too! (5) **A / An** small animal. It's (6) **a / an** snake. (7) **A / An** orange snake.

It's horrible! And I can see (8) **a / an** dog. (9) **A / An** small dog. (10) **A / An** English dog. And I love it!

## 5 School things

► SB, p. 21

a) **Look at the pictures. Write the words from the box.**
*Schau dir die Bilder an. Schreibe die Wörter aus dem Kästchen auf.*

| book • case • desk • glue • pen • pencil • rubber • ruler • sharpener |
|---|

1 
a pencil ...

2 
a pencil ...

3 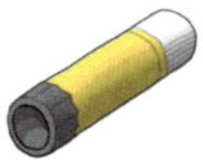
a ... stick

4 

5 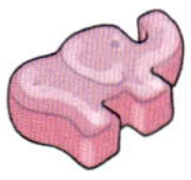

6 
an exercise ...

7 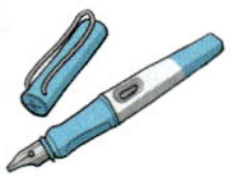

8 

9 

b) **Right (✓) or wrong (✗)?**
*Richtig (✓) oder falsch (✗)?*

1 The ruler is purple. ☐
2 The pencil is brown. ☐
3 The rubber is an elephant! ☐
4 The pencil case is green and black. ☐
5 The pencil sharpener is a dog! ☐
6 The pen is blue and white. ☐

## 6 What can you see?

► SB, p. 21

**Look at the picture.**
**Complete the sentence.**
*Schau dir das Bild an.*
*Ergänze den Satz.*

**!** one pen → two pens

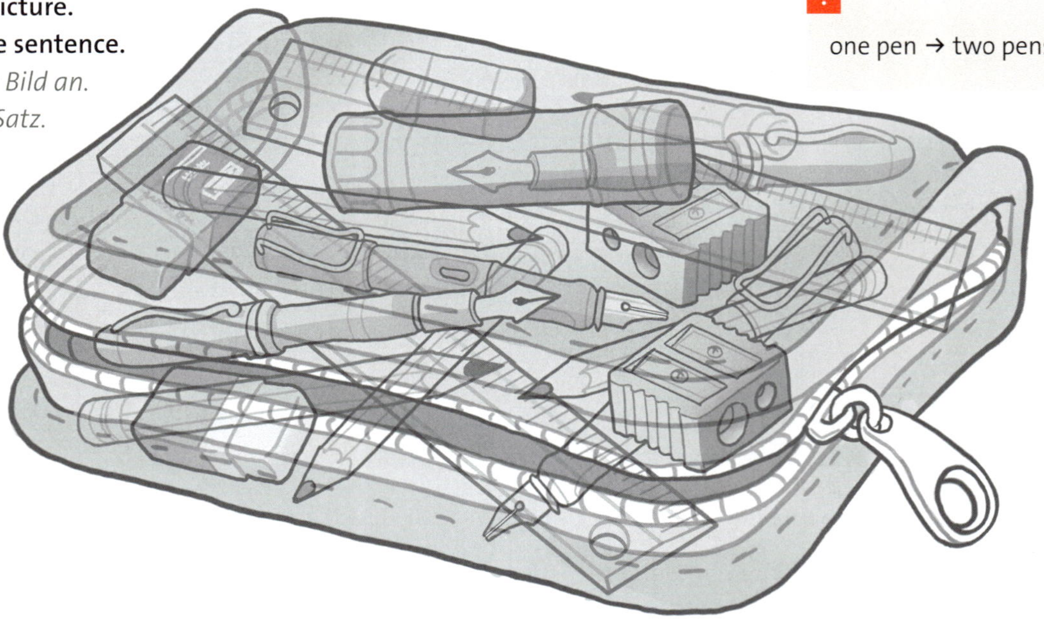

In the pencil case there are two pencil sharpeners, one glue three

## 7 Questions in an English lesson class

▸ Digital help ▸ SB, p. 23

**a) Write the words in the right order.** *Schreibe die Wörter in der richtigen Reihenfolge auf.*

1 I / use / pencil / please / Can / your / ?

Can ______ please?

2 window / open / Can / the / I / please / ?

______

3 What's / answer / question / the / to / five / ?

______

4 it / is / page / What / ?

______

5 exercise three / help / Can / me / with / you / ?

______

**b) Look at the pictures. Which question from a) goes with picture A? Which one goes with picture B?**
*Sieh dir die Bilder an. Welche Frage aus a) passt zu Bild 1? Welche zu Bild 2?*

1

2

## 8 We're all new in this school!

▸ SB, p. 24

**Write the correct words from the box.**
*Schreibe die richtigen Wörter aus dem Kästchen auf.*

| I • you • he • she • we • they |
|---|

I can understand and use classroom English.

Erklär-
film

## 9 LANGUAGE *to be* Break at Varndean School

▸ SB, p. 24

**Write the correct words from the box.**

*Schreibe die richtigen Wörter aus dem Kästchen auf.*

| |
|---|
| I'm • you're • he's • it's (2x) • she's (2x) • they're • we're |

## 10 Days of the week

► SB, p. 25

a) **Find and highlight six days of the week and write them.**
*Finde und markiere sechs Wochentage und schreibe sie auf.*

SUTMONDAYYRETUESDAYOSATWEDNESDAYFRYTHURSDAY FRIDAYMASATRSUNDAY

______________________________________________

______________________________________________

b) **Now write the missing day.** *Nun schreibe den fehlenden Tag auf.* ______________________

## 11 Yasmin's lessons at Pelham School

► SB, p. 26

02

a) LISTENING **Listen to five lessons in a different school. What subjects do you hear? Write 1–5 next to the subjects.** *Höre dir fünf Unterrichtsstunden in einer anderen Schule an. Welche Fächer hörst du? Schreibe 1–5 neben die Schulfächer.*

| | | | | |
|---|---|---|---|---|
|  |  |  |  |  |
| **English** ☐ | **maths** 1 | **music** ☐ | **science** ☐ | **French** ☐ |
| Tuesday, Thursday, Friday | Monday, Thursday, Friday | Tuesday | Monday, Wednesday, Friday | Monday, Wednesday |
|  |  |  |  | 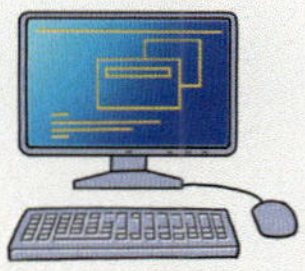 |
| **history** ☐ | **geography** ☐ | **PE** ☐ | **design & technology** ☐ | **computing** ☐ |
| Wednesday | Monday, Friday | Tuesday, Thursday | Thursday | Friday |

b) SPEAKING **Look again at Yasmin's timetable in 11a). What subjects are on what days? Practise with a partner.** *Sieh dir Yasmins Stundenplan nochmals an. Wann werden welche Fächer unterrichtet? Übe mit einer Partnerin / einem Partner.*

Partner A: *Maths is ...* — *on Monday, Thursday and Friday.* :Partner B

Partner B: *And PE is ...* — *on Tuesday and Thursday.* :Partner A

## 12 LISTENING The timetable in Pelham School

▸ SB, p. 27

03 a) **Listen to Daniel's timetable on Monday and Tuesday. Circle the right words.**
*Höre dir Daniels Stundenplan von Montag und Dienstag an. Umkreise die richtigen Wörter.*

| Monday | Tuesday | Wednesday | Thursday | Friday |
|---|---|---|---|---|
| maths | maths |   |  | 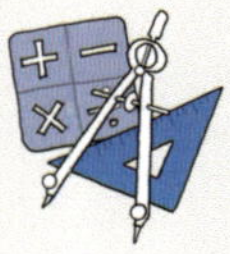 |
| science / art | history / maths |  | 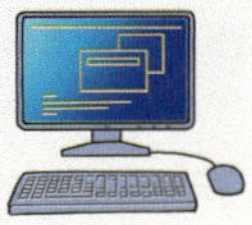 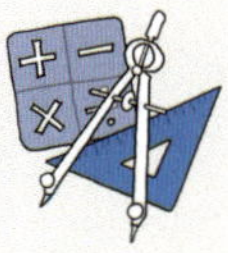 |  |
| break | break | break | break | break |
| English | geography | 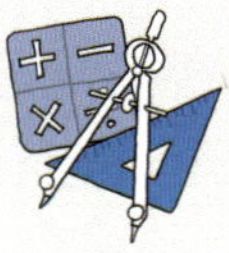 |   |  |
| lunch | lunch | lunch | lunch | lunch |
| French / PE | design and technology / English |   | 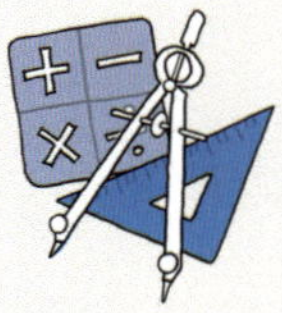 |   |

04 b) **Now listen to Daniel's timetable on Wednesday, Thursday and Friday. Circle the right pictures.**
*Nun höre dir Daniels Stundenplan von Mittwoch, Donnerstag und Freitag an. Umkreise die richtigen Bilder.*



I can write my timetable in English.

## ☒ 13 What about you?

▸ SB, p. 27

**What do you like? What don't you like? Write four sentences.**

*Was magst du? Was nicht? Schreibe vier Sätze.*

| | | | |
|---|---|---|---|
| I like<br>I don't like | science:<br>drawing:<br>swimming:<br>my friends:<br>school uniforms:<br>holidays:<br>elephants: | it's<br>they're | horrible.<br>clever.<br>hard.<br>cool.<br>nice.<br>big. |

1 *I like holidays: they're cool.*

2 ____________________

3 ____________________

4 ____________________

5 ____________________

## 14 Places in school

▸ Digital help ▸ SB, p. 28

**Show a friend the places in school. Write the missing words.**

*Zeige einer Freundin / einem Freund die Orte in der Schule. Schreibe die fehlenden Wörter auf.*

art • building • canteen • computer • favourite • hall

A

This is the sports _ _ _ _.

B

This is the _ _ _ room.

C

History and music are in this _ _ _ _ _ _ _ _.

D

This is the _ _ _ _ _ _ _. We have lunch here.

E

This is the _ _ _ _ _ _ _ _ room.

F

And this is my _ _ _ _ _ _ _ _ _ place – I love swimming!

## 15 LANGUAGE *to be* (negative) Lunchtime at Varndean School

► SB, p. 29

Erklär-film

**Circle the right verb forms.** *Umkreise die richtigen Verbformen.*

## 16 LANGUAGE *to be* (positive and negative)

► SB, p. 29

**Write the right forms of *to be*.**
*Schreibe die richtigen Formen von* to be *auf.*

are (2x) • aren't • isn't • 'm • 's

1 We ________ tired!

2 We ________ happy.

3 I ________ scared.

4 The students ______ in the sports hall.

5 It ________ a pencil.

6 She ________ lucky!

I can describe my school.

## 17 READING People in the story

▸ SB, pp. 30–31

**Look at the story on pages 30–31 in your book. Write the name or names.**
*Schau dir die Story auf den Seiten 30-31 an. Schreibe den oder die Namen auf.*

Jade • Kyle • Lily (2x) • Noah (2x) • Sunita • Zane

1 He's busy. ______
2 They're bullies. ______
3 He's in trouble. ______
4 She's scared of Kyle and Jade at first. ______
5 They talk to the bullies. ______
6 He's good with animals. ______

## 18 READING Right or wrong?

▸ SB, pp. 30–31

**Read sentences 1–6. Are they right (✓) or wrong (✗)?**
*Lies die Sätze 1–6. Sind sie richtig (✓) oder falsch (✗)?*

1 Zane isn't free after school. ☐
2 Kyle and Jade are mean to Noah. ☐
3 Lily and Sunita help Noah. ☐
4 Kyle and Jade like Scout. ☐
5 Lily and Sunita are good friends to Noah. ☐
6 Buddy is Noah's brother. ☐

## 19 READING Language in the story

▸ SB, pp. 30–31

**Match the words in red with the words in blue. Write the sentences.**
*Ordne die roten Wörter den blauen zu. Schreibe die Sätze auf.*

| | |
|---|---|
| Let's go | him! |
| Who | with animals. |
| He's | to the beach. |
| Let's help | meet you. |
| You're good | are they? |
| Nice to | in trouble. |

1 ______
2 ______
3 ______
4 ______
5 ______
6 ______

I can understand a story about friends. ✓

## 20 Match the parts

a) **Match the parts in blue with the parts in black. Draw lines.**
*Ordne den Teilen in Blau die passenden Teile in Schwarz zu. Ziehe Linien:*

| | |
|---|---|
| I' m | busy. |
| I have | an exercise book. |
| | 11 years old. |
| | from Germany. |
| | an apple. |
| | late. |

b) **Now write the six sentences – in English and then in German.**
*Schreibe nun die sechs Sätze auf – auf Englisch und dann auf Deutsch.*

1 ____________________
2 ____________________
3 ____________________
4 ____________________
5 ____________________
6 ____________________

## 21 The right letters

**Complete the words with the letters *ie, ou, ea* or *ow*.**
*Ergänze die Wörter mit den Buchstaben* ie, ou, ea *oder* ow.

1 Dana is my fr____nd. She's nice. *(page 31)*
2 And that's Mr Carter. He's my t____cher. *(page 22)*
3 I don't like my school uniform. I don't like t____s! *(page 20)*
4 We have sc____nce on Tuesday and Thursday. *(page 26)*
5 Can I open the wind____? *(page 22)*
6 Pl____se sit d____n. *(page 22)*
7 My fav____rite sport is park____r. *(page 19)*
8 Is the canteen n____r the art room? – I don't kn____. *(pages 28, 23)*

Brauchst du Hilfe? Du findest die Wörter auf den Seiten, die hinter den Sätzen in Klammern angegeben sind.

## 22 Which word is wrong?

**Write the wrong word.** *Schreibe das Wort auf, das nicht passt.*

1 two eight Wednesday fifteen — *Wednesday*

2 lion dog ruler snake — ____________

3 map grey blue white — ____________

4 football parkour swimming cooking — ____________

5 science French hall history — ____________

6 canteen classroom sports hall biology — ____________

7 drawing building coding cooking — ____________

## 23 SPEAKING Speak good English

05

a) **Listen to the words. Then listen again and repeat them.**
*Höre dir die Wörter an. Dann höre noch einmal zu und wiederhole sie.*

1 -**i**- as in six: stick British building minutes history
2 -**i**- as in five: like goodbye right design nice Hi!

b) **Write the words in the box in the right list.** ▸ Digital help
*Schreibe die Wörter in dem Kästchen in die richtige Liste.*

| -**i**- as in six | -**i**- as in five |
|---|---|
| *favourite* | ____________ |
| ____________ | ____________ |
| ____________ | ____________ |
| ____________ | ____________ |
| ____________ | ____________ |

~~favourite~~ • Friday • I'm • lion • my • opposite • pink • science • swim • this

06

c) **Now say these sentences to your partner. Then listen and check your pronunciation.** *Sage diese Sätze deiner Partnerin / deinem Partner. Dann höre zu und überprüfe deine Aussprache.*

1 We have design on Friday.
2 Hi, my nice white lion! Bye!
3 History is my favourite subject.
4 I'm right!
5 Mike is nice.
6 We have six minutes of swimming.
7 I like science.

## I think English is:

fun ☐ hard ☐ OK ☐

## My favourite words:

*seagull*

## My favourite character:

## Difficult words:

*friends*

## My favourite phrases:

*Here you are!*

## I remember:

Lessons: *art,*

Places in school: *hall,*

Questions in class: *What page ist it?*

Words to describe people: *helpful,*

## Learning English:

Complete the smileys: ☺ = I like it. 😐 = It's OK. ☹ = I don't like it.

Speaking ◯ Listening ◯ Viewing ◯

Writing ◯ Story ◯ Learning words ◯

## 1 A quiz on Unit 1

a) **Find the answers in your Lighthouse student's book. Write your answers.**
*Suche die Antworten in deinem Schulbuch. Schreibe deine Antworten auf.*

1 The name of your English book: __ __ __ __ __ __ __ __ __ __

2 The colours of the Varndean school uniform: red, white, __ __ __ __ *(page 20)*

3 How many students in the photo? __ __ __ __ *(page 20)*

4 A word beginning with Q: __ __ __ __ __ __ __ __ *(page 23)*

5 A day with nine letters: __ __ __ __ __ __ __ __ __ *(page 25)*

6 Two subjects beginning with a vowel (A, E, I, O, U): art and __ __ __ __ __ __ __ *(page 26)*

7 Find a word with ten letters: __ __ __ __ __ __ __ __ __ __ *(page 28)*

b) **Make the right word with the yellow letters in a).**
*Setze die gelb markierten Buchstaben aus a) zu einem Wort zusammen.*

Kyle and Jade are ______________ *(page 30)*

## 2 WRITING As many sentences as you can

► Digital help

**Write as many sentences as you can about Lily. Start all the sentences with *She's* ...**
*Schreibe so viele Sätze wie du kannst über Lily. Beginne alle Sätze mit* She's ...

1 *She's Lily.* ______________
2 *She's eleven.* ______________
3 *She's* ______________
4 *She's* ______________
5 *She's at Varndean School.* ______________
6 *She's* ______________
7 ______________
8 ______________

*Can you write five or more sentences? You can find information about Lily in this unit, for example on pages 19, 20, 29, 30, 31 and 32.*

► Check

# Unit 2
# My family and home

## 1 Oscar and his family

▸ SB, p. 45

a) **Oscar is a student in 7C at Varndean School. Write about his family.**
*Oscar ist Schüler in Klasse 7C an der Varndean Schule. Schreibe über seine Familie.*

aunt • brother • cousin • grandpa • sister

Hi, I'm Oscar. My s________ is Olivia. Freddie is my b________. My mum's sister is my a________ Jane. Amelia is my c________. I have two grandmas and one g________.

b) **Look again at Oscar's family in a). Then complete the sentences with: *name + 's*.**
*Sieh dir Oscars Familie in a) nochmals an. Ergänze die Sätze mit Name + 's.*

1 Oscar's mum is Jane's sister.
2 Olivia is Freddie and ________ sister.
3 Freddie is Oscar and ________ brother.
4 Jane is ________ mum.
5 Amelia is ________ cousin.

I can talk about my family.

## 2 An animal puzzle

▶ SB, p. 46

**Look at the photos and read the sentences. Write the animal words in the plural.**
*Sieh dir die Fotos an und lies die Sätze. Schreibe die Tiere im Plural auf.*

1 We say *Meow*! *Meow*! We are c____________.

2 We are small brown pets. We are h____________.

3 We are loud and say *Woof*! *Woof*! We are d____________.

4 We are big. We are brown, black or grey. We are h____________.

5 We swim and swim and swim. We are f____________.

6 We are orange and blue. We are p____________.

7 We say *Sssss! Sssss!* People are scared of us! We are s____________.

8 We hop – hop – hop! We are r____________.

## 3 George isn't happy!

▶ SB, p. 46

a) **Write the missing words.** *Ergänze die fehlenden Wörter.*

because • house • I'm • It's • messy • of • quiet

*1 Hello, __________ George. __________ the weekend and I'm not happy.*
*2 I live in Sunita's ____________.*
*3 I'm not happy because there are a lot ______ animals in the house.*
*4 We have a lot of animals __________ Meera is a vet.*
*5 I'm angry because the animals are loud, not __________.*
*6 And I'm not happy because the house is __________.*

b) **Now check with your partner.** *Überprüfe die Sätze mit deiner Partnerin / deinem Partner.*

Erklär-film

## 4 LANGUAGE Short answers All about you

▸ SB, p. 47

**Answer the questions. Use the answers in the box.**
*Beantworte die Fragen. Nutze die Antworten in dem Kasten.*

| Yes, I am. • Yes, we are. • No, I'm not. • No, we aren't. |
|---|

1 Are you a girl? – ______________________

2 Are you a boy? – ______________________

3 Are you 11 years old? – ______________________

4 Are you German? – ______________________

5 Are you and your friends football fans? – ______________________

6 Are you and your friends in Berlin? – ______________________

**!**
Are you OK?
– Yes, I am. / No, I'm not.
Are you OK?
– Yes, we are. / No, we aren't.

## 5 LANGUAGE Questions and short answers Varndean School

▸ SB, p. 47

**Complete the questions with *is* or *are*. Write short answers.**
*Ergänze die Fragen mit* is *oder* are. *Schreibe Kurzantworten.*

1 Is Mr Lee a class teacher? – Yes, he is.

2 ________ Mr Lee also a maths teacher? – he isn't.

3 ________ Lily in 7F? – ______________________

4 ________ Sunita and Noah in 7C? – ______________________

5 ________ Zane in a band? – ______________________

6 ________ Kyle and Jade friends of Noah? – No, ______________________

**!**
Is he OK?
– Yes, he is. / No, he isn't.
Is she OK?
– Yes, she is. / No, she isn't.
Are they OK?
– Yes, they are. / No, they aren't.

## 6 George, the parrot

▸ SB, p. 47

**Put six apostrophes (') in the orange places. Two orange places stay empty.**
*Ergänze sechs Apostrophe an den orangefarben markierten Stellen. Zwei Stellen bleiben leer.*

Hi, I●m George, Sunita●s parrot.
We have a lot of animal●s from
Meera●s work in the house. She●s a vet.
Are the animal●s quiet? No, they aren●t!
This isn●t a good house for a parrot.

## 7 LISTENING Questions and answers about pets

07

► SB, p. 49

a) **Oscar asks his friends about their pets. Listen twice: First listen and circle the right answer. Then listen again and check your answers.**
*Oscar fragt seine Freunde und Freundinnen nach ihren Haustieren. Höre zweimal zu: zuerst höre zu und umkreise die richtige Antwort. Dann höre noch einmal zu und überprüfe deine Antworten.*

*It's ok if you don't understand every word.**

*Es ist OK, wenn du nicht jedes Wort verstehst.*

1 Zara says dogs are too loud / difficult.

2 Oscar says Molly has an interesting name / colour.

3 Noah says Daisy is very fast / very old.

4 Ava says her hamster is one year old / two years old.

b) **Listen again and tick (✓) the right answer.** *Höre noch einmal zu und hake die richtige (✓) Antwort ab.*

1 Leo the lizard is ...

A loud. ☐
B big. ☐
C very friendly. ☐

2 Molly the cat is ...

A very active. ☐
B always hungry. ☐
C big. ☐

3 Daisy the dog is ...

A cute. ☐
B loud. ☐
C very fast. ☐

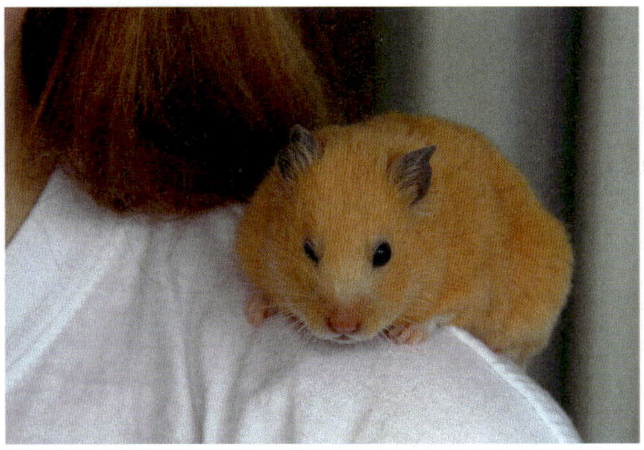

4 Harry the hamster is ...

A messy. ☐
B very interesting. ☐
C not very active. ☐

I can talk about pets.

## 8 Oscar's new flat

▸ SB, p. 51

a) **Write the missing words.** *Ergänze die fehlenden Wörter.*

Our new ___ ___ ___ ___ is in this house.

It's on the top ___ ___ ___ ___ ___ of the house.

There are three big ___ ___ ___ ___ ___ in the ___ ___ ___ ___ ___ ___.

We have nice ___ ___ ___ ___ ___ ___ ___ ___ ___ ___ on the ground floor.

b) **Now look at the plan of Oscar's flat. Write the correct words from the box.**
*Nun schau dir den Plan von Oscars Wohnung an. Ergänze die Wörter aus dem Kasten.*

| area • bathroom • bedroom (3x) • kitchen • living room |
|---|

1 ______________________

2 ______________________

3 dining ______________________

4 Olivia's ______________________

5 Oscar and Freddie's ______________________

6 ______________________

7 mum and dad's ______________________

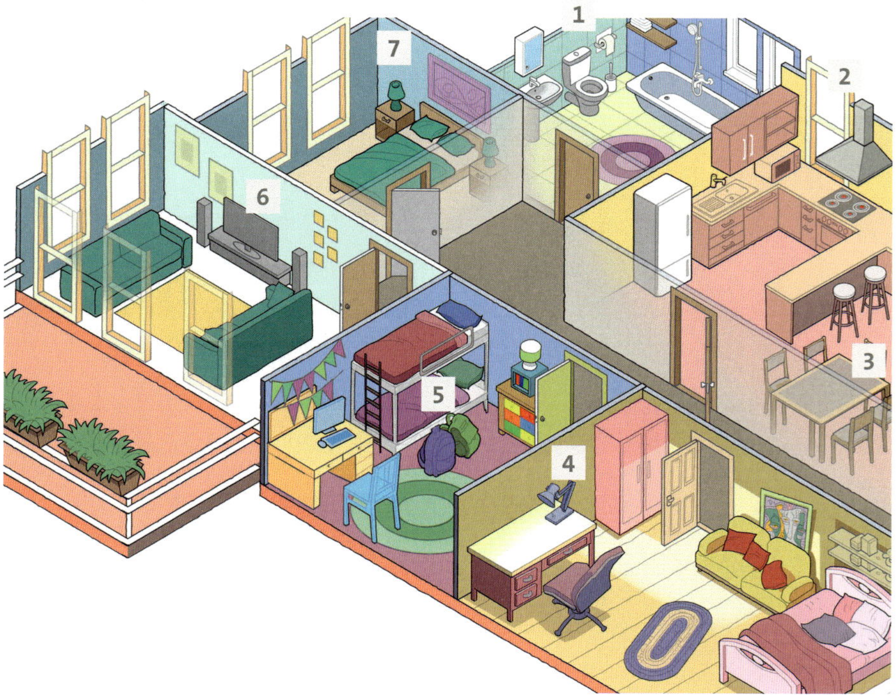




I can describe my home or dream home.

## 9 The rooms in Oscar's flat

► SB p. 51

a) **Look at the pictures and complete the sentences.**
*Sieh dir die Bilder an und ergänze die Sätze.*

**!**
There's + singular: There's a cat here.
There are + plural: There are two cats here.

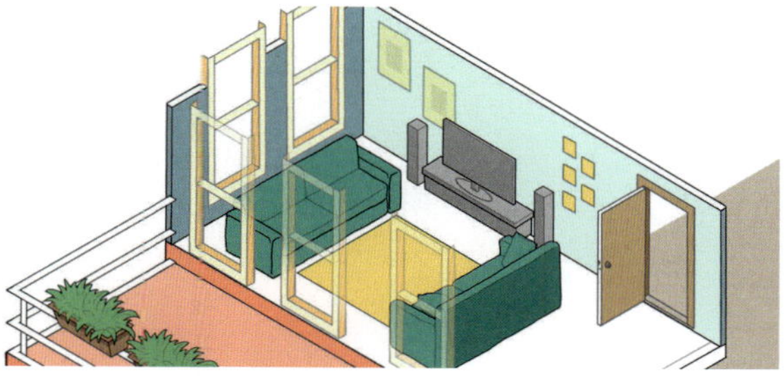

1 There's a [ ] _ _ _ _ _ _ _ _ _ _ _.

2 There are three _ _ _ _ [ ] _ _ _.

3 There's a _ [ ] _ _ _ _ _
with a dining _ _ _ _ .

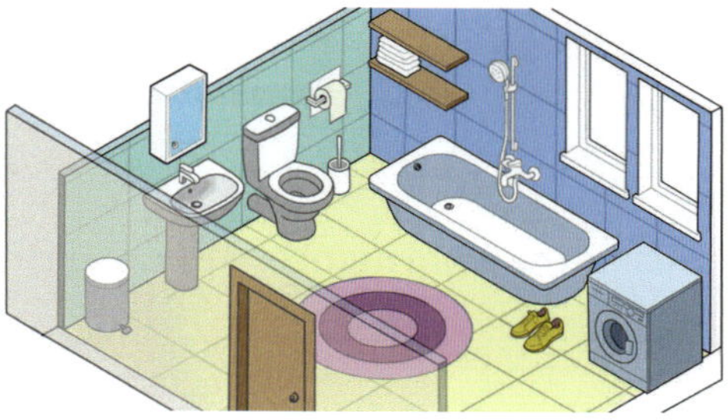

4 There _ a _ _ [ ] _ _ _ _ _ _.

5 There _ a _ _ _ _ [ ] _ with three big [ ] _ _ _ _ .

b) **Make a word from the letters in the boxes. It's a place in a house or flat.**
*Bilde ein Wort aus den Buchstaben in den Kästen. Es ist ein Ort in einem Haus oder einer Wohnung.*

The word is: ____________________

c) **Answer the questions.** *Beantworte die Fragen.*

1 Where are the shoes? In the ____________________

2 Where is the table? ____________________

3 Where are the sofas? ____________________

## 10 Things in a room

► SB, p. 52

a) **Look at the pictures. Write the seven words in the puzzle.**
*Schau dir die Bilder an. Schreibe die sieben Wörter in das Kreuzworträtsel.*

1 

2 

3 

4 

5 

6 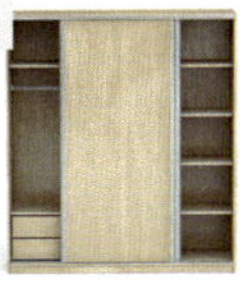

7 

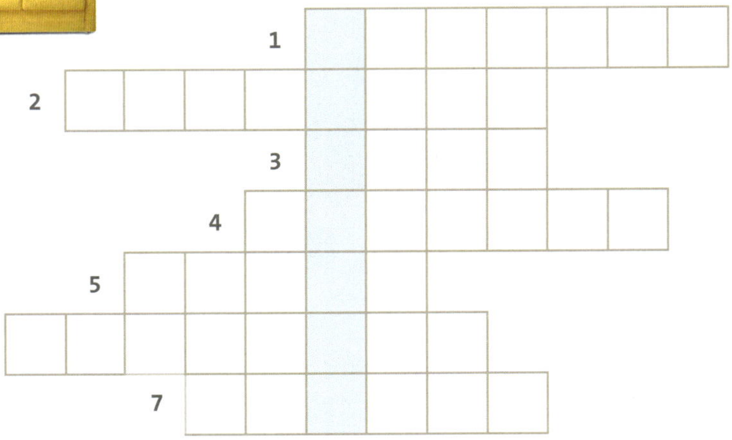


b) **What is the word number 8?** *Was ist Wort Nummer 8?*

______________

**Draw a picture of it in the box.**
*Male ein Bild davon in den Kasten.*

## ☒ 11 Oscar's room

► SB, p. 52

**Oscar writes about his room. Write words 1–8 correctly.**
*Oscar beschreibt sein Zimmer. Schreibe die Wörter 1-8 richtig auf.*

My room is (1) ______________, but very nice.

It's on the first (2) ______________ of our house.

In my room I have my (3) ______________ and a big brown wardrobe.

My (4) ______________ and shoes are in the (5) ______________.

And I have a (6) ______________ and a chair too.

I have a computer, some (7) ______________ and three posters of my favourite stars.

And I have a nice new (8) ______________.

| | |
|---|---|
| 1 | SALML |
| 2 | FOLOR |
| 3 | EDB |
| 4 | COTHELS |
| 5 | WORDRABE |
| 6 | TLBAE |
| 7 | BOKOS |
| 8 | LMAP |

I can describe my room.

## ☒ 12 Olivia's room

► SB, p. 54

**Sentences 1–5 are wrong. Look at the picture and correct them. Use words from the box.**
*Sätze 1-5 sind falsch. Schau dir das Bild an und korrigiere sie. Verwende Wörter aus dem Kasten.*

| behind • in front of • next to • on • under |
|---|

1 Olivia's shoes are on the bed.
No, they aren't ! They are ______ the bed

2 The chair is behind the table.
No, it isn't! It's ______

3 Her red cushions are on the bed.
No, they ______ They are ______

4 Her shelves are next to the door.
No, ______

5 The picture is under the sofa.
______

## 13 Questions and answers

► SB, p. 54

**First read the answers. Then write the missing question words.**
*Lies zuerst die Antworten. Dann ergänze die fehlenden Fragewörter.*

1 ______ is Olivia? – Olivia is Oscar's sister.

2 ______'s Oscar and Olivia's flat? – It's in Brighton.

3 ______'s behind the flat? – A garden with three big trees.

4 ______'s Olivia's bedroom? – Next to Freddie and Oscar's room.

5 ______'s Olivia's favourite thing in her room? – Her phone.

!
What? - a thing
Where? - a place
Who? - a person

## ☒ 14 Reading At grandma's house

▸ Digital help ▸ SB, p. 55

**Read Oscar's text and the questions. First highlight the places in the text where you find the information for your answers. Then write the answers to the questions.** *Lies Oscars Text und die Fragen. Markiere zuerst die Stellen im Text, die die gesuchten Informationen enthalten. Dann schreibe die Antworten auf.*

*My mum's mum has a house in Watford, near London. I love my grandma's house. It isn't very big, but it's very old and really nice. The hall has six doors! On the ground floor my grandma has a living room with a big window and you can see three big trees in her garden. She has a kitchen with a dining area, but we often eat in the garden because my grandma likes barbecues.*

*My grandma has a dog, Monty.*

*Monty is a funny animal and I like to play with him. Monty loves the big old sofa in my grandma's living room and he always wants to play with my shoes!*

*There are really nice neighbours on one side, but horrible neighbours on the other side. I'm a bit scared of the horrible neighbours. They're mean.*

*When I'm at my grandma's house I have a room on the first floor, next to the bathroom. When I'm not there, it's my grandma's office. In the room there are shelves with a lot of interesting books. My grandma loves reading. Her favourite books are history books.*

*My grandma always has some chocolate for me when I come. She is a very special person for me.*

1 Is grandma's house modern? *No, (it's) very old.*

2 What's special in the hall? ______

3 What is there in grandma's garden? ______

4 Are all the neighbours friendly? ______

5 Where is Oscar's room in grandma's house? ______

6 What are on the shelves in grandma's office? ______

7 What are grandma's favourite books? ______

8 Grandma always has something special for Oscar. What is it? ______

## 15 READING Sunita and Ben

▶ SB, pp. 56–57

**Look at the story on pages 56–57 in your book. Answer the questions about the four parts.**
*Schau dir die Geschichte auf den Seiten 56-57 in deinem Buch an. Beantworte die Fragen zu den vier Teilen.*

*The start of the story ...*

1 Where's Sunita at the start of the story? ______________________.

2 Is Sunita a fan of Ben? Yes, because he's funny and ______________________.

No, because his music is ______________________.

3 Who loves Ben's music? ______________________.

*In the dining room...*

4 What's true? Tick (✓) A or B.

A Nish and Sunita have a lot of homework. ☐ B Nish and Sunita think Ben's music is really bad. ☐

*Later in the living room ...*

5 What are two problems with Ben's music? It's bad and ____________.

6 What's the end of the problem?

Ben can use headphones and he can ______________________.

*The end of the story (in Sunita's texts to Lily) ...*

7 Where can Sunita use some of Ben's music? ______________________.

## 16 READING All about Ben

▶ SB, pp. 56–57

**Write the missing words.** *Schreibe die fehlenden Wörter auf.*

Ben is *a*__________ in the living room with his *g*__________. And his *m*__________ is loud and horrible!

But he can use *h*__________ and he can help Sunita with music for her video *g*__________.

## 17 READING Language in the text

▶ SB, pp. 56–57

**Find the opposites in the story.** *Finde die Gegensätze in der Geschichte.*

1 with other people ◂▸ *a*__________

2 loud ◂▸ *q*__________

3 there ◂▸ *h*__________

4 really great ◂▸ *h*__________

5 small ◂▸ *b*__________

6 old ◂▸ *n*__________

7 good ◂▸ *b*__________

8 no ◂▸ *y*__________

I can understand a problem and talk about it.

## 18 Words in Unit 2

**Write the words in the right list.** *Schreibe die Wörter in die richtige Liste.*

~~angry~~ • ~~aunt~~ • bedroom • brother • chair • cook • cousin • cushions • dining area • hall • kitchen • living room • messy • neighbour • polite • quiet • shelves • table • tidy • tired • vet • wardrobe

| people | about a person | places in a flat | things in a room |
|---|---|---|---|
| *aunt* | *angry* | ______ | ______ |
| ______ | ______ | ______ | ______ |
| ______ | ______ | ______ | ______ |
| ______ | ______ | ______ | ______ |
| ______ | ______ | ______ | ______ |
| ______ | ______ | | |

## 19 Words that are nearly the same

**Write the right words in the sentences.** *Ergänze die richtigen Wörter in den Sätzen.*

1 her/here — My cousin Alice is with us ______ in our house. I like ______

2 four/for — I have ______ chairs and some shelves ______ my books.

3 two/too — And I have ______ tables ______.

4 red/read — I use my nice ______ lamp when I ______.

5 its/it's — My lamp is old, but ______ special. I like ______ colour.

## 20 Questions

**Draw lines and match the questions and answers.**
*Zeichne Verbindungslinien und ordne die Fragen und Antworten einander zu.*

1 Are you OK?
2 Is your school OK?
3 Where is your home?
4 Who is at home with you?
5 What is your favourite hobby?
6 Why are you tired?

a In Brighton.
b Because my homework is hard.
c Yes, I am.
d My dad, my stepmum and my brother.
e Yes, it is.
f Swimming.

## 21 Where is Scout?

**Write the right words.**
*Ergänze die richtigen Wörter.*

behind • in • in front of • next to • under

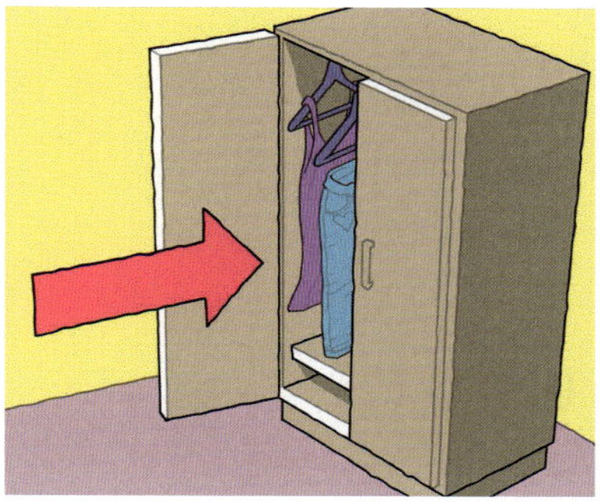

1 Is Scout ______________ the wardrobe?
– No, she isn't!

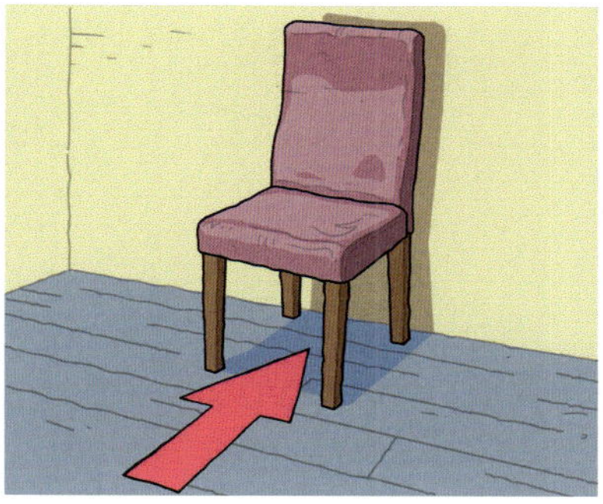

2 Is she ______________ the chair?
– No, she isn't!

3 Is she ______________ the table?
– No, she isn't!

4 Is she ______________ the sofa?
– No, she isn't!

5 She is ______________ the door!

## 22 Listening and Speaking Speak good English

08

a) **Listen to these six words. What's special about the letters in blue?**
*Höre dir diese sechs Wörter an. Was ist das Besondere an den blau markierten Buchstaben?*

1 listen 2 answer 3 know
4 chocolate 5 interesting 6 two

b) **Look at the following sentences. Highlight the letters that you don't say.** *Schau dir die folgenden Sätze an. Markiere die Buchstaben, die du nicht sprichst.*

1 That's interesting, but it's also wrong.
2 What's the right answer?
3 My friends like walking and talking!
4 My grandma lives in a different building.
5 I know eight different people in this class.

09

c) **Listen to the sentences and repeat them.** *Höre dir die Sätze an und wiederhole sie.*

### I think English is:

not hard ☐ quite hard ☐
very hard ☐ fun ☐
interesting ☐ useful ☐

### My favourite page in Unit 2:

___

### Why:

___

___

### My favourite words:

dream ___

___

___

___

### Difficult words:

| to write: | to say: |
| --- | --- |
| neighbour | clothes |
| ___ | ___ |
| ___ | ___ |
| ___ | |

### I remember:

Family: parents, ___

___

Rooms in the house: hall, ___

___

Question words: who?, ___

Where things are: under, ___

Adjectives to describe people: cute, ___

### Learning English:

Complete the smileys: ☺ = I like it. 😐 = It's OK. ☹ = I don't like it.

Speaking ○ Listening ○ Viewing ○
Writing ○ Story ○ Spelling ○

## 1 Word puzzles

Can you complete the puzzles? Write one letter in each box.
*Kannst du die Rätsel ergänzen? Schreibe einen Buchstaben in jedes Kästchen.*

a) Words to describe people and things
*Wörter um Menschen und Sachen zu beschreiben*

| | | | | | | | | | |
|---|---|---|---|---|---|---|---|---|---|
| 1 | S | A | D | | | | | | |
| 2 | T | | | | | | | | |
| 3 | A | | | | | | | | |
| 4 | H | | | | | | | | |
| 5 | F | | | | | | | | |
| 6 | D | | | | | | | | |

1 not happy
2 not messy
3 not with other people
4 when you want to eat
5 not mean
6 hard

b) Verbs *Verben*

| | | | | | | | | |
|---|---|---|---|---|---|---|---|---|
| 1 | E | A | T | | | | | |
| 2 | P | | | | | | | |
| 3 | D | | | | | | | |
| 4 | A | | | | | | | |
| 5 | B | | | | | | | |
| 6 | R | | | | | | | |

1 have a sandwich or other food
2 you ... football, a game, the guitar
3 see pictures when I'm asleep
4 after a question you ...
5 (*two words*) not be wrong
6 think of a thing again

c) Family – you choose the words!
*Familie - du bestimmst die Wörter!*

| | | | | | | | |
|---|---|---|---|---|---|---|---|
| 1 | | | | | | | |
| 2 | | | | | | | |
| 3 | | | | | | | |
| 4 | | | | | | | |

d) Things in a bedroom – you choose!
*Dinge in deinem Schlafzimmer - du suchst aus!*

| | | | | | | | | |
|---|---|---|---|---|---|---|---|---|
| 1 | S | O | F | A | | | | |
| 2 | | | | | | | | |
| 3 | | | | | | | | |
| 4 | | | | | | | | |

## 2 A message in code

Sunita is at school. Her phone buzzes. It's a message from Lily – a message in code!
Can you write the message? *Sunita ist in der Schule. Ihr Handy klingelt. Es ist eine Nachricht von Lily - eine verschlüsselte Nachricht! Kannst du sie aufschreiben?*

| |
|---|
| +^. ^ ∗{ ]∗□↕ ⌂—/ ꟻ>+——]. □↕]] □+↕ □↕∗ >+↕/ {ɷ |
| Hi. I TELL |
| /∗±±^□ ^ꟻ ]—ꟻ□ ^ῷ □+↕ "∗/<↕ῷ. □+∗ῷ=ꟻ. |
| |

| ∗ | | | | ↕ | | | + | ^ | | | ] | | | — | | / | ꟻ | □ | ɷ |
|---|---|---|---|---|---|---|---|---|---|---|---|---|---|---|---|---|---|---|---|
| A | B | C | D | E | F | G | H | I | J | K | L | M | N | O | P | R | S | T | Y |

► Check

# Unit 3
# My day

## 1 Oscar

▸ SB, p. 77

**a) Write Oscar's sentences (1–5).**
*Schreibe Oscars Sätze auf.*

!
I go to ... by ...
I walk to ...

**1** Picture: ☐

by • go • grandma's house • I • to my • train

*I go to my* ____________________
*by* ____________________.

**2** Picture: ☐

by • car • dad's flat • go • I • to my

*I go to* ____________________
*by* ____________________.

**3** Picture: ☐

beach • bike • by • go • I • to the

____________________
____________________.

**4** Picture: ☐

friend's house • I • to my • walk

____________________
____________________.

**5** Picture: ☐

bus • by • go • I • school • to

____________________
____________________.

**b) Match the pictures (A–E) with the sentences (1–5). Write the letters in the boxes.**
*Ordne die Fotos (A-E) den Sätzen (1-5) zu. Schreibe die Buchstaben in die Kästchen.*

A

B

C

D

E

I can talk about my school journey.

## 2 LISTENING **Numbers**

▸ Digital help ▸ SB, p. 78

10–13

a) • **Choose five numbers: 10 15 20 25 30 35 40 45 50 55 60. Write them in the boxes.**
*Wähle fünf Zahlen aus. Schreibe sie in die Kästchen.*

• **Play the game in groups. Listen. When you hear your numbers, cross them out ~~(15)~~.**
*Spielt das Spiel in Gruppen. Hört zu. Wenn ihr eure Zahlen hört, streicht sie durch.*

• **When you have all five numbers, shout "Here!". The game ends – you win!**
*Wenn ihr alle fünf Zahlen habt, ruft „Here!". Das Spiel ist zu Ende - ihr gewinnt!*

Game 1

| | | | | |
|---|---|---|---|---|
| | | | | |

Game 3

| | | | | |
|---|---|---|---|---|
| | | | | |

Game 2

| | | | | |
|---|---|---|---|---|
| | | | | |

Game 4

| | | | | |
|---|---|---|---|---|
| | | | | |

14

b) **Listen. Circle the right number.** *Höre zu. Umkreise die richtige Zahl.*

| | | | |
|---|---|---|---|
| 1 34/43 | 2 25/52 | 3 64/46 | 4 54/45 |
| 5 42/24 | 6 36/63 | 7 26/62 | 8 53/35 |

!
43 dreiundvierzig
43 forty-three

## 3 LANGUAGE **Simple present Oscar's Saturday**

▸ SB, p. 80

Erklär-film

**Write a sentence for each picture.** *Schreibe zu jedem Bild einen Satz.*

| | |
|---|---|
| He does his homework. | He has a shower. |
| He watches TV. | He eats breakfast. |
| He plays football. | He gets up. |
| He gets dressed. | He goes to the park with his sister. |

1 
______________________
______________________

2 
______________________
______________________

3 
______________________
______________________

4 
______________________
______________________

5 
______________________
______________________

6 

______________________
______________________

7 
______________________
______________________

8 
______________________
______________________

## 4 Funny sentences

▸ SB, p. 80

**The verbs in the sentences are wrong! Write the correct verbs.**
*Die Verben in den Sätzen sind falsch. Schreibe die richtigen Verben auf.*

! brush → brushes

1 At 7 a.m. Molly ~~eats~~ *has* ________ a shower.
2 Then she ~~does~~ ________ dressed.
3 And then she ~~has~~ ________ her teeth.
4 At 1 p.m. she ~~plays~~ ________ lunch.
5 In the afternoon she ~~brushes~~ ________ the shopping.
6 And then she ~~gets~~ ________ football.

## 5 LANGUAGE Simple present Oscar's mum and dad

▸ SB, p. 80

a) **Find the times. Write sentences about Saturday. Write the verbs in the simple present.**
*Finde die Uhrzeiten. Schreibe Sätze über den Samstag. Setze die Verben ins simple present.*

*he / she + 's:*
*play → plays / do → does / go → goes*

1 Oscar's mum / get up
2 She / phone / her mum
3 She / go / swimming
4 Oscar's dad / make / breakfast
5 He / meet / some friends
6 He / do / the shopping

at 9.15 a.m.
at 7.05 a.m.
at 8.30 p.m.
at 10.30 a.m.
at 7.45 p.m.
at 7.25 a.m.

1 *Oscar's mum gets up at* ________
2 *She* ________
3 ________
4 ________
5 ________
6 ________

b) **Check with your partner.** *Überprüfe mit deiner Partnerin / deinem Partner.*

*Oscar's mum gets up at seven oh five a.m.*

*Right.*

*Wrong.*

## 6 LANGUAGE **Simple present** **Oscar's friend Ling**

▸ SB, p. 80

a) **Ling tells Oscar about her week. Circle the correct verb.**
*Ling erzählt Oscar von ihrer Woche. Umkreise das richtige Verb.*

| | | Time |
|---|---|---|
| 1 | On weekdays I **get / gets** up at 7 a.m. and I **have / has** a shower. | **7.05 a.m. / 7.10 a.m.** |
| 2 | My mum **make / makes** breakfast for me and my brothers. | **7.20 a.m. / 7.25 a.m.** |
| 3 | I **walk / walks** to school and my parents **goes / go** to work by car. | **8.10 a.m. / 8.20 a.m.** |
| 4 | But on Sunday we **make / makes** breakfast for mum and dad. | **9.30 a.m. / 9.45 a.m.** |
| 5 | My grandma **is / are** with us on Sundays from 11.30. | **11.15 a.m. / 11.30 a.m.** |
| 6 | She **make / makes** my favourite lunch! | **12 o'clock / 1 o'clock** |
| 7 | Then we all **play / plays** games. It's nice! | |
| 8 | I **love / loves** Sundays! | |

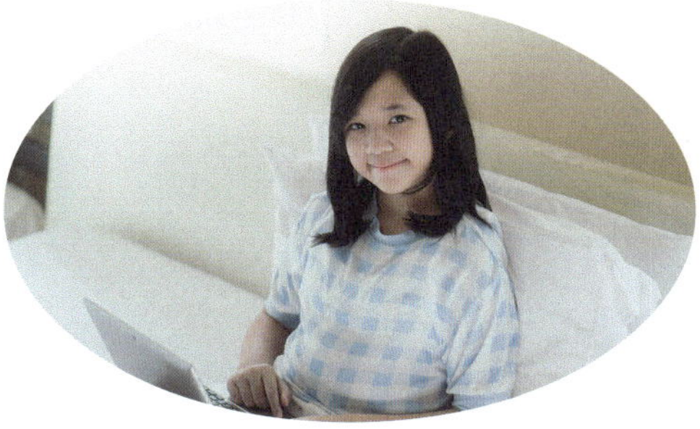

15
b) **Listen and check your answers.**
*Höre zu und überprüfe deine Antworten.*

15
c) **Listen again and circle the correct times.**
*Höre noch einmal zu und ergänze die Zeiten.*

## 7 LANGUAGE **Simple present** **Kitty, the cat**

▸ SB, p. 80

**Ling's cat Kitty talks about her day! Write the verbs in the simple present.**
*Lings Katze Kitty erzählt von ihrem Tag. Setze die Verben ins simple present.*

I (1 get) ______________ up at 6 o'clock. It's very quiet.
The mum (2 make) ______________ my breakfast at 7 o'clock,
and Ling (3 play) ______________ with me before school.

In the afternoon, I often (4 watch) ______________ seagulls
in the garden.
The big seagull (5 have) ______________ a lot of friends.
Then I (6 go) ______________ to bed.

In the evening, I (7 eat) ______________ my dinner.
Then Ling (8 brush) ______________ me – prrrr!

I can describe my daily routine.

## 8 Sports and hobbies

▸ SB, p. 82

a) **Complete the sports and hobbies with *a, e, i, o, u*.** *Ergänze die Sportarten und Hobbys mit* a,e,i,o,u.

1 r__nn__ng    2 cr__ck__t    3 y__g__    4 t__bl__ t__nn__s

5 d_nc__ng    6 w__nds__rf__ng    7 s__ng__ng    8 c__mp__t__r g__m__s

9 __rt    10 w__lk__ng    11 p__rk__ __r    12 tr__mp__l__n__ng

b) **Now write the correct words from a) in the poster.** *Nun schreibe die richtigen Wörter aus a) in das Poster.*

### *Bridgecross Secondary School*

We have lots of clubs at our school. Join a club – everybody is welcome!

When? – The clubs meet: ▲ at lunchtime ● after school

Where? – Look online, on the school's *Clubs* website.

Monday

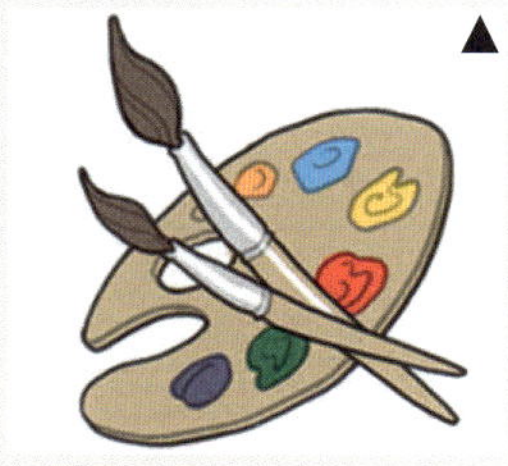
▲ ____________

● ____________

● ____________

● ____________

Wednesday

▲ ____________

▲ ____________

● ____________

● ____________

c) MEDIATION **A friend asks you about the school clubs. Answer the questions in German.**
*Ein Freund befragt dich zu den Schul-AGs. Beantworte die Fragen auf Deutsch.*

1 Was bedeuten die Symbole ▲ und ●?

▲ = ____________________

● = ____________________

2 Wie findet man heraus, wo die AGs stattfinden?

____________________

## 9 Do you go running?

► SB, p. 83

**Read the sentences. Write the names in the right order.**
*Lies die Sätze. Schreibe die Namen in der richtigen Reihenfolge auf.*

Mo: *I always go running.*
Holly: *I often go running.*
Reeta: *I sometimes go running.*
Ben: *I never go running.*

1 Ben
2 ______
3 ______
4 ______

## 10 Are you a good detective?

► SB, p. 83

a) **Write these sentences.**
*Schreibe diese Sätze auf.*

A I ofttɘn go ɔyɔling. ↔ I often
B Mum lovɘƨ tɒking qhotoƨ. ↔ ______
C Ɑɒb nɘvɘɿ goɘƨ ƨwimming. ↔ ______
D I bon't likɘ hoɔkɘy. ↔ ______

E Dad often plays basketball. — Dad
F We sometimes go surfing. — ______
G I always listen to music. — ______
H Mum and I often do drawing. — ______

b) **Write the sports and hobbies and the correct letters (A–H) from part a).**
*Schreibe die Sportarten und Hobbys und die richtigen Buchstaben (A-H) aus Aufgabe a) auf.*

1  E — basketball
2  ☐ — ______
3  ☐ — ______
4  ☐ — ______
5  ☐ — ______
6  ☐ — ______
7  ☐ — ______
8  ☐ — ______

## 11 Reading Online chat room

▶ SB, p. 85

**a) Read the messages. Are the sentences true (✓) or false (✗)?**
*Lies die Nachrichten. Sind die Sätze richtig oder falsch?*

*Hello. My name is Connor and I live in Hove. I often play cricket and basketball, and I go running with my sister. I sometimes go windsurfing. It's great! I like books too – I love science-fiction.*

*Hi! I'm Sophia and I'm 11. I go to a hockey club after school with my friend. I like it – the other kids are nice. My dad and I often go cycling at the weekend.*

*Hey! I'm Becky and I'm 12. I really like playing computer games and I go to a club after school. I sometimes go swimming – it's fun. I live in Brighton, but I never go swimming in the sea. What about you? Tell me about your hobbies!*

*Hello. My name is Luke and I'm 10. After school, I always play my guitar in my bedroom. I like singing too. I sometimes play table tennis with my friends. My friend Joel has a table at his house.*

| | | | True | False |
|---|---|---|---|---|
| 1 | a | Becky plays computer games. | ☐ | ☐ |
| | b | She often goes swimming in the sea. | ☐ | ☐ |
| 2 | a | Connor does a lot of sport. | ☐ | ☐ |
| | b | He likes books. | ☐ | ☐ |
| 3 | a | Sophia plays hockey at the weekend. | ☐ | ☐ |
| | b | She often goes cycling. | ☐ | ☐ |
| 4 | a | Luke likes music. | ☐ | ☐ |
| | b | He never plays table tennis with his friends. | ☐ | ☐ |

**b) Write a message for the chat room.**
*Schreibe eine Nachricht für den Chatroom.*

play football/basketball/ the guitar • watch TV • do art • listen to music • play computer games • ...

Hi, I'm ______________________ *(your name)* and I'm ____________ *(how old?)*.

I often ______________________________________________.

Sometimes I ______________________________________________.

And I love ______________________________________________.

But I never ______________________________________________.

I can talk about my free time.

## 12 Listening Radio interviews on the beach

16

► SB, p. 85

a) **Listen to the people. Find the right picture. Write the letter (A–F).**
*Höre den Leuten zu. Finde das richtige Bild. Schreibe den Buchstaben (A-F) auf.*

Listen again if you need to.

1 Picture: ________
2 Picture: ________
3 Picture: ________
4 Picture: ________
5 Picture: ________
6 Picture: ________

A

B

C

D

E

F

b) **Listen again. Circle the right word.** *Höre noch einmal zu. Umkreise das richtige Wort.*

1 sometimes / often / always
2 sometimes / always / often
3 often / sometimes / always
4 always / often / sometimes
5 often / always / sometimes
6 always / sometimes / often

## 13 Free time

► SB, p. 85

a) **Write five sentences about your partner.** *Schreibe fünf Sätze über deine Partnerin / deinen Partner.*

| | | | |
|---|---|---|---|
| You | like<br>don't like | drama cooking singing windsurfing trampolining art music ... | |
| | sometimes<br>often<br>never | play | football the guitar computer games table tennis ... |
| | | go | cycling walking running swimming dancing ... |
| | | watch TV<br>listen to music | |

______________________________________________

______________________________________________

______________________________________________

______________________________________________

______________________________________________

b) **Now say your sentences to your partner. Are they right or wrong?**
*Nun sage deine Sätze deiner Partnerin / deinem Partner. Sind sie richtig oder falsch?*

*You sometimes play football.*

*Wrong! I never play football.*

## 14 Listening Friends want to meet

17 ► SB, p. 86

**Listen to these friends. Right (✓) or wrong (✗)?** *Höre diesen Freunden zu. Richtig oder falsch?*

| | | | ✓ / ✗ |
|---|---|---|---|
| A | 1 | Max is free on Sunday. | ✗ |
| | 2 | Anna wants to go to the beach. | ______ |
| | 3 | They meet at 11.30. | ______ |
| B | 1 | Lucy has drama club on Saturday. | ______ |
| | 2 | Dev wants to go to walking. | ______ |
| | 3 | Their meeting is at Lucy's house. | ______ |

## 15 Speaking Are you free?

► Digital help ► SB, p. 86

**Look at the diagram. Act four conversations with a partner. Use words from boxes 1–4. You can use your own ideas too! Swap roles.** *Schaut das Diagramm an. Spielt vier Unterhaltungen mit einer Partnerin / einem Partner. Nutzt die Wörter in den Kästen 1-4. Ihr dürft auch eigene Ideen nutzen. Tauscht die Rollen.*

A: Are you free on (1)? Let's (2).

B: Good idea! I'd love to. → A: Great!

B: Sorry, I can't. I'm busy. → A: What about (1)?

B: OK. Let's meet at (3).

A: Where? At (4)?

B: OK. See you.

(1) Friday / Saturday / Sunday / Monday / ...

(2) go walking / go swimming / go to the cafe / play table tennis / watch a film / ...

(3) 2 o'clock / 3 o'clock / ...

(4) my house / my flat / your house / your flat / ...



I can make plans to meet friends.

## 16 VIEWING Who helps?

► SB, p. 91

**Watch the video again. Circle the right words.**
*Schau dir das Video noch einmal an. Umkreise die richtigen Wörter.*

1 Emir talks to Gloria. Gloria has a **good / bad** idea.
2 Daisy phones Amal. Amal **can / can't** help her.
3 Daisy goes to Gloria's house. Gloria is busy **today / at the weekend**.
4 Jenny gives Daisy her **guitar / skateboard**.
5 Daisy's brother Kieran gives Daisy an idea because his music is **loud / quiet**.

## 17 VIEWING You can act

► SB, p. 91

a) **Watch Part 1 (00:39 to 01:15) again and read the text. Listen to *how* they say the sentences.**
*Schau den ersten Teil noch einmal und lies den Text. Höre wie sie die Sätze sagen.*

**Emir** You want me to play my next football match with a pair of underpants on my head?!? Like this? Are you crazy[1]?!?
**Daisy** And you want me to play street music? Street music?!? In front of people? I can't sing. I can't play a musical instrument! How can I do street music?
**Emir** Dare or no dare?
**Daisy** Dare!

b) SPEAKING **Now act the part with a partner. Act it lots of times so you're really good!**
*Nun spielt diesen Teil zu zweit. Übt viele Male, damit ihr richtig gut seid!*

You can watch again and say the sentences after Emir and Daisy.

## 18 What do you think?

► SB, p. 91

**Write what you think about the dares. You can use words from the box.**
*Schreibe auf, was du über die Wetten denkst. Du kannst Wörter aus dem Kasten verwenden.*

a good idea • great • mean • really funny • too hard • weird • ...

1 I think Emir's dare for Daisy is ______________________
2 I think Daisy's ______________________

[1] **crazy** *verrückt*

## 19 The odd word out

**Which is the odd word out? ~~Cross it out~~.** *Welches Wort past nicht? Streiche es durch.*

1. car, journey, bike, train
2. husband, son, brother, neighbour
3. competition, book, newspaper, comic
4. pound, euro, prize, dollar

## 20 Feelings

**Complete the sentences under the pictures. Use the words from the box.**
*Ergänze die Sätze unter den Bildern. Verwende die Wörter aus dem Kasten.*

| angry • happy • sad • scared • surprised • tired |
|---|

1 
The boy is ____________.

2 
The woman is ____________.

3 
The kids are ____________.

4 
The dog is ____________.

5 
The girl is ____________.

6 
The man is ____________.

## 21 Opposites

**Write the opposites of these words and phrases.**
*Schreibe die Gegenteile dieser Wörter und Wendungen auf.*

1 always ◄► ____________ 2 a.m. ◄► ____________ 3 start ◄► ____________

4 mean ◄► ____________ 5 after ◄► ____________ 6 go to bed ◄► ____________

## 22 Important little words

**Akbar talks about Friday. Circle the right words.**
*Akbar erzählt vom Freitag. Umkreise die richtigen Wörter.*

**On / In** Friday lessons at my school end **on / at** 1 p.m. It's great!

I always see my friend Millie **in / at** the afternoon.

We meet **at / by** my house and we often go **at / to** the park.

We play football **on / in** the park with some other kids.

We sometimes go **to / at** the beach **by / in** bus.

I like swimming **on / in** the sea!

## 23 Useful phrases

**Oscar asks Ling to go to the beach. Complete the useful phrases with words from the box.**
*Oscar bittet Ling mit an den Strand zu gehen. Ergänze die useful phrases mit Wörtern aus dem Kasten.*

| about • best • done • let's • of • sorry |
|---|

| | |
|---|---|
| Oscar | Are you free on Sunday? __________ go to the beach. |
| Ling | Sorry, I'm busy. I have a lot ______ homework. |
| Oscar | Oh, OK. What __________ Saturday? |
| Ling | Sorry, I can't. But don't be __________ for me – I'm in a singing competition. It's the final! |
| Oscar | That's great! Well __________ ! |
| Ling | Thanks, Oscar - that helps me. You're the __________ ! |

## 24 SPEAKING Speak English well

a) **Look at the words.**
**Find the 'Zane' words [eɪ]. Circle them.**
**Find the 'dad' words [æ]. Underline them.**
*Schau dir die Wörter an.*
*Finde die ‚Zane' -Wörter. Umkreise sie.*
*Finde die ‚dad'-Wörter. Unterstreiche sie.*

dad Zane snack
plan skateboard trampolining pay
take badminton hat game

**Zane**
**[eɪ] in your dictionary**

**Dad**
**[æ] in your dictionary**

18 b) **Listen and check. Repeat the words.** *Höre zu und prüfe. Wiederhole die Wörter.*

**My favourite words:**

o'clock

**Difficult words:** | **to write** | **to say**

| Difficult words | to write | to say |
| --- | --- | --- |
| teeth | ☐ | ☑ |
| | ☐ | ☐ |
| | ☐ | ☐ |
| | ☐ | ☐ |

**Useful phrases:**

I'd love to.

**I remember:**

How people go to school: by car,

In the morning: I get up,

Some hobbies and activities: trampolining,

Some things I do: I watch ... / I go ... / I like ... / ...

How often: always,

**My favourite exercises in Unit 3 in the workbook:**

Write the exercise numbers:

**My progress[1] in English:**

- ☐ great!
- ☐ OK
- ☐ some things are hard

[1] **progress** *Fortschritt*

## 1 Twelve different girls

▸ Check

**Partner game: Partner A says four sentences about one girl. Then partner B looks at the pictures. How fast can partner B find the right girl? Then swap.** *Partnerspiel: Partnerin A / Partner A sagt vier Sätze über ein Mädchen. Dann schaut sich Partnerin B / Partner B die Bilder an. Wie schnell findet sie/er das richtige Mädchen? Dann tauscht.*

| | |
|---|---|
| She lives in a | flat house. |
| She has | cat dog fish parrot. |
| She likes | art computer games cricket cycling dancing hockey running swimming trampolining walking windsurfing yoga. |

Eva

Orla

Pari

Pippa

Rosa

Hannah

Penny

Aarna

Carmen

Tamara

Tess

Noor

## 1 Opposites[1]

**Write the opposites. Pick the right words from the box.**

▸ Digital help

great • loud • mean • old • slow • short • small • wrong

1 long ◂▸ _ _ _ _ _
2 quiet ◂▸ _ _ _ _
3 new ◂▸ _ _ _
4 right ◂▸ _ _ _ _ _
5 big ◂▸ _ _ _ _ _
6 fast ◂▸ _ _ _ _
7 friendly ◂▸ _ _ _ _
8 horrible ◂▸ _ _ _ _ _

## 2 Tia's friends

**Complete the sentences with *am, are, aren't* or *is*.**

Is Susi tired?
– Yes, she _______.

Are Ela and Miran in a bus?
– No, they _______.

_______ you happy, Lisa?

Yes, I _______.

## 3 Tia's hamsters

**Read sentences 1–8. Look at the picture of Tia's bedroom on page 55. Find Tia's hamsters. Write the correct letters.**

1 Pip is a small, black hamster. It's on Tia's bed. __________
2 Pop is a white hamster. It's on the floor, next to the wardrobe. __________
3 Hammy is under the bed. It's scared! __________
4 Speedy is a big, brown hamster. It's on a cushion on the floor. __________
5 Rambo is on the floor, next to the guitar. __________
6 Cookie is a brown hamster. It's on the shelf next to the window. __________
7 Blackie is a black hamster. It's on the wardrobe! __________
8 Muffin is on the chair, next to the desk. __________

[1] **opposite** *Gegenteil*

▸ Check

Erklär-
film

## 4 Tia's hobbies

Look at Tia's room again. Can you find: ☐ 4 + hobbies / ☒ 6 hobbies? Write sentences.

*She plays* ______________________

______________________

______________________

**!** Remember: *she* ... +*s*
*I like* → *she likes*
*I play* → *she plays*

*She likes* ______________________

______________________

______________________

______________________

______________________

► Check

# Unit 4
# Where I live

## 1 Places in a city

► SB, p. 105

a) Write the seven places.

A

This is a

s ___ ___ ___.

B

This is a

___ ___ ___ ___ ___ ___ ___.

C

This is a

___ ___ ___ i ___ ___.

D

This is a

p ___ ___ ___.

E

Here are nice

___ ___ ___ ___ ___ ___ ___.

F

This is a

s ___ ___ ___ ___ ___.

G

And here is the

___ ___ ___ ___ h.

b) Complete Scout's sentence with the yellow letters.

*I like fi______ and ch______.*

## 2 Activities in Brighton

► SB, p. 105

Write the verbs. Use the verbs in the box.

| |
|---|
| do • eat • go • listen • play • watch |

| | | |
|---|---|---|
| You ... | ____________ | films. |
| | ____________ | fish and chips. |
| | ____________ | games. |
| | ____________ | bowling. |
| | ____________ | to music. |
| | ____________ | skateboarding. |

I can understand information about Brighton.

## 3 LISTENING Our neighbourhoods

19

▸ SB, p. 106

a) Five students in class 7C talk about their neighbourhoods.
Listen and read the texts.

**Fatima**
*Hi, my name is Fatima and I live on a farm near Brighton. It's a nice place to live. I can often go walking in the country with my mum and dad. I like that. And we have two shops in the village, where we can buy food. So yeah, I like where I live. The people here are friendly.*

**Finley**
*OK, I'm Finley and live on an estate in Brighton. It's OK, we have a good youth centre with cool activities. I like going there. Sometimes it's loud where we live – cars go too fast and people have loud music. But not always. It's OK.*

**Hannah**
*Hi, I'm Hannah and I live in a flat in the centre of Brighton. We have a lot of shops near us, that's great, but I don't really like it here. There are a lot of people, it's very loud and there's a lot of rubbish everywhere. Why can't people take their rubbish home?*

**Ivy**
*So, I'm Ivy and I live with my mum and my brother (and my dog!) on an estate in Brighton. We live in a flat on the top floor. It's OK, we have shops and we're lucky, we're near a big park where I can go walking with my dog. But, well, you can't do much here really, so it can be a bit boring here ... sometimes ....*

**Syed**
*Hi, my name is Syed and I live on an estate and I like it here. My friends live here. We have lots of places where we can play football together, but there's often a lot of rubbish there. That's stupid. Me and my friends, we just want to play football there.*

b) Now listen again. What do the students talk about? Put a tick (✓) in the right boxes.

| | estate | shops | youth centre | outdoor activities | loud? | rubbish |
|---|---|---|---|---|---|---|
| Fatima | | | | | | |
| Finley | | | | | | |
| Hannah | | | | | | |
| Ivy | | | | | | |
| Syed | | | | | | |

c) Listen again and (circle) the right words.

1 Fatima says the people in her neighbourhood are **friendly / unfriendly**.

2 Finley **likes / doesn't like** the activities in the youth centre.

3 Hannah **likes / doesn't like** her estate.

4 Ivy lives with her mum and **sister / brother**.

5 Syed wants to **play football / ride his bike**.

## 4 LANGUAGE Simple present: negative sentences School

► SB, p. 107

a) **Read about school in Britain. Then write about school in Germany.**
**Put the words in blue in the right order.**

|  |  |
|---|---|
| 1 School often starts at 8.50 am. | *School doesn't start at 8.50 a.m.*<br>**start / at 8.50 a.m. / doesn't / school** |
| 2 Most students have a uniform. | **have / a uniform / students / don't** |
| 3 The school day often starts with assembly. | **the school day / start with / doesn't / assembly** |
| 4 Students have lunch at school. | **most students / at school / have lunch / don't** |
| 5 Students have lessons after lunch. | **most students / have lessons / don't / after lunch** |
| 6 Students often play cricket. | **play / cricket / students / don't** |

b) **Now write about the students at Varndean School. Circle *doesn't* or *don't*.**

Lily and Noah **doesn't / don't** (1) walk to school because they **doesn't / don't** (2) live near Varndean.

Lily and her family **doesn't / don't** (3) have a car. So Lily **doesn't / don't** (4) go to school by car.

She goes by bike. Zane **doesn't / don't** (5) go to school by bike like Lily. He walks.

The end of school is at 3.05, but a lot of students **doesn't / don't** (6) go home then. Lily sometimes goes to homework club, but Zane **doesn't / don't** (7) like homework club.

## 5 Language Simple present: negative sentences Lily's neighbourhood

▸ SB, p. 107

**Now read about Lily's neighbourhood.**
**Circle the right form of the verb.**

> *Remember!*
> *My friend George **lives** in Sunita's house.*
> *He **doesn't live** in Zane's house.*

1 Lily Hall **live / lives** on the Whitehawk Estate.
 She doesn't **live / lives** near the beach.
2 She **go / goes** to Homework Club when her dad doesn't **come / comes** home before 5 o'clock.
3 Lily's neighbour **walk / walks** with his dog, but Lily doesn't **have / has** a dog.
4 Lily sometimes **walk / walks** in the country with her dad, but he doesn't **walk / walks** very often.
5 Lily **like / likes** her estate because it doesn't **have / has** a lot of problems.
6 But she doesn't **like / likes** all the rubbish and all the cars in her estate.

## 6 Language Simple present: negative sentences Alina

▸ SB, p. 107

**Read about Alina, a student at Varndean School. Then complete the sentences.**
**Use the verbs in blue in the negative with *don't* and *doesn't*.**

1 We live in a flat.
We *don't live* ______
in a house.

2 I have a cat.
I ______
a dog.

3 My mum works in a school.
She ______
in a shop.

4 I feel happy.
I ______ sad.

5 My sister lives in London.
She ______
with us.

6 My dad plays football, but
he ______
cricket.

I can describe my neighbourhood.

## 7 Lily and the homework club

▶ SB, p.108

**Read the text on page 108 in your student's book. Then read sentences 1–8. Are the sentences right (✓) or wrong (✗)?**

1 Lily goes to the homework club on Tuesday. ☐
2 You can do crafts at the homework club. ☐
3 There's a girls' group on Tuesday. ☐
4 Lily goes to the girl's group every Tuesday. ☐
5 Niles is Lily's neighbour. ☐
6 Lily pays for homework club. ☐

## 8 Places in town

▶ SB, p. 110

**Highlight seven places in town. Then write the seven places below.**

1 *hospital* 2 ______ 3 ______ 4 ______
5 ______ 6 ______ 7 ______

Erklär-film

## 9 LANGUAGE Simple present: questions Oscar and Chandra

▶ SB, p. 111

**Chandra asks Oscar some questions and Oscar answers. Circle the right word in the questions.**

1 **Does / Do** you all live in a house? – No, we don't. We live in a flat.
2 **Does / Do** your grandma live with you? – No, she doesn't.
3 **Does / Do** your sister Olivia share a room? – No, she doesn't.
4 **Does / Do** you have posters in your room? – Yes, I do.
5 **Does / Do** your flat have a dining area? – Yes, it does.
6 **Does / Do** you like school, Oscar? – No, I don't.

## 10 LANGUAGE Simple present: short answers Now you

► SB, p. 111

a) Chandra asks you some questions. Write your answers. Use short answers.

1 Do you all live in a village?

– *Yes, we do. / No, we don't.*

2 Do you like your neighbourhood?

– ______________________

3 Does your school have a lot of students? – ______________________

4 Do you go to school by bike? – ______________________

5 Does your house or flat have a garden? – ______________________

6 Do you sometimes go bowling? – ______________________

**!**
Do you …? – Yes, we do. / No, we don't.
– Yes, I do. / No, I don't.
Does it …? – Yes, it does. / No, it doesn't.

b) SPEAKING Your partner asks you questions 1–6 and you answer. Then swap roles.

## 11 LANGUAGE Simple present: questions Your questions to Chandra

► SB, p. 111

**Put the words in the right order and write your questions under the right pictures.**

1 walk / you / do / to school / ?
2 have / you / do / a nice room / ?
3 your dog / like / the garden / does / ?
4 your mum / does / work / in the garden / ?

A

______________________

B

______________________

C

______________________

D

______________________

## 12 Language Simple present: questions and short answers Devon and York

▸ SB, p. 112

Partner B: Look at page 86.
Partner A: You want to know:
Is Devon a good place for a holiday in England?

a) Write the questions about Devon. Put the words in the right order.

1 have / does / Devon / good windsurfing / ?
*Does Devon have* ______________________ ☐

2 many big cities / Devon / does / have / ?
______________________ ☐

3 Devon / does / good beaches / have / ?
______________________ ☐

4 good places for walking / does / have / Devon / ?
______________________ ☐

5 good / does / Devon / have / football clubs / ?
______________________ ☐

b) Now ask your partner about Devon. Put a tick (✓) in the box for yes, an (✗) for no.

c) Now look at the information about York.

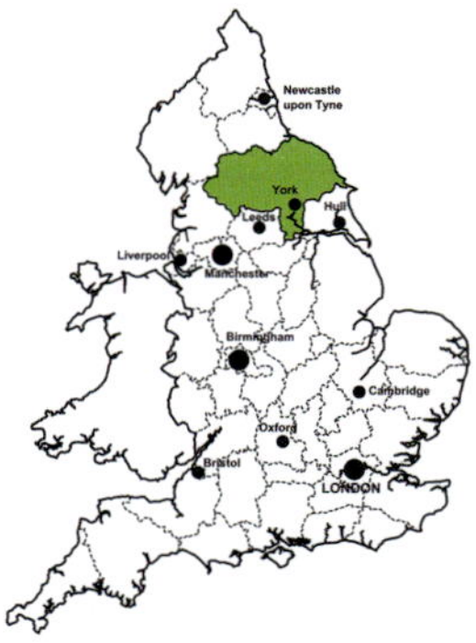


York has many old buildings, interesting shops and a great train museum.
But York doesn't have a marina, a beach or a big football stadium.

d) Your partner asks you about York.
Answer your partner's questions. Use short answers: *Yes, it does. / No, it doesn't.*

e) Now check your answers with your partner.

## 13 LISTENING A weather map

20

▶ SB, p. 114

a) Listen and look at the map.
Circle one right weather symbol in each town.

**Key**

sunny

cloudy

windy

rainy

snowy

cold

warm

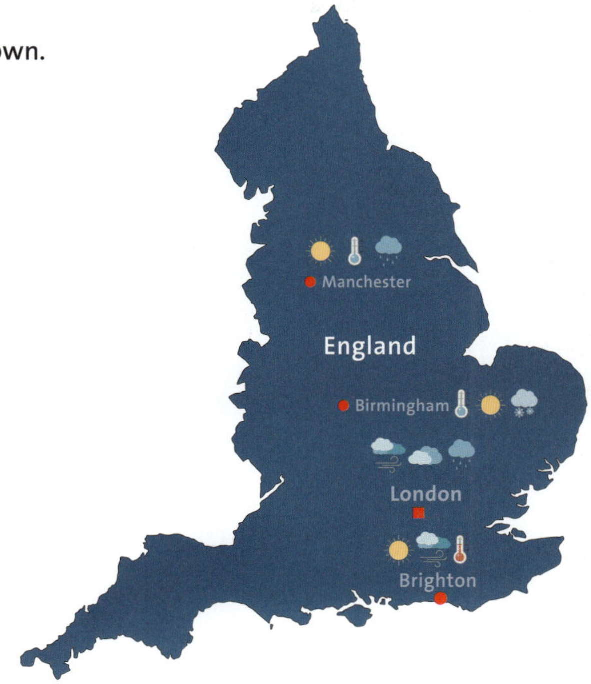


b) Listen again. Write the last word in each sentence.

1 In London it is very rainy in the afternoon and ______________ .

2 In Brighton it's a great day for the ____________________ .

3 In Manchester it's a different _______________________ .

4 In Birmingham it's a good day to be inside with a nice hot ______________ .

## 14 A funny old train

▶ SB, p. 114

Brighton has the oldest electric train in the world.
Match questions 1–6 with answers A–F.

1 When does it open? _____

2 How long is the journey? _____

3 Where does the journey start? _____

4 What does the journey cost? _____

5 How often do the trains go? _____

6 Does the train take dogs? _____

A *It's very short! There are only three stops.*

B *£3.95 or £2.45 for girls and boys up to 15.*

C *Yes, it does, and the dogs travel free.*

D *At Aquarium Station.*

E *Every 15 minutes.*

F *At 11.30 on Monday and Wednesday, and at 10.30 on other days.*

I can talk about sights in Brighton and the weather.

## 15 A great place to work

▶ SB, p. 115

a) Oscar writes about his dad's work for school. Read his text and the brochure.

*My dad Kevin has a great job. He helps visitors in Thorpe Park, a fantastic fun park near London with great rollercoasters. Visitors can travel at 80 miles per hour (128 kilometres per hour) on Stealth. Or they can travel upside down on Vortex. My dad goes to work at 6.45 am, but he likes his work because he can sometimes ride on Stealth and Vortex when the visitors go home.*

**Thorpe Park**

A park where all the family can have fun.

Fish and chips.

A day ticket isn't expensive.

Bring guide dogs for free.

Do you have a question? Please call us.

b) Highlight the words in the text and brochure that mean:

1 people who come to the park
2 go fast
3 head down
4 parents with their kids
5 have a great time
6 hot food
7 doesn't cost a lot
8 don't pay
9 want to ask something

Erklär-film

c) LANGUAGE Simple present: ***wh***-questions
Write the questions.

1 *Where* *does* Kevin work? – He works at Thorpe Park.

2 ______ ______ Kevin do? – He helps the visitors.

3 ______ fast ______ visitors travel on *Stealth*? – They travel at 80 miles per hour.

4 ______ ______ visitors travel on *Vortex*? – They travel upside down.

5 ______ ______ Kevin go to work? – He goes to work at 6.45.

6 ______ ______ Kevin like his job? – Because he can sometimes go on *Stealth* and *Vortex*.

## 16 Reading Tell the story

▶ SB, pp. 116–117

**Look at the story on pages 116–117 in your book. Then match the questions 1–6 with the answers A–F.**

1 What do the people on the estate do? ___
2 Where do they meet? ___
3 Who is angry? ___
4 What does Buddy do? ___
5 When do the neighbours meet for lunch? ___
6 What does Lily talk about at lunch? ___

A At 12 o'clock.
B He digs and finds a ring.
C They have a clean-up day.
D About the ring.
E Mr Davies.
F In front of the youth centre.

## 17 Reading Wrong information in the story

▶ SB, pp. 116–117

**One word is wrong in each sentence. Write the correct word.**

1 On Sunday morning there's a big group in front of the ~~library~~. *youth centre*
2 It's clean-up day because people don't want to live on a ~~noisy~~ estate. ______
3 Buddy finds a dead mouse, an old ~~hat~~ and a gold ring. ______
4 At 12 o'clock the neighbours have over ~~twenty~~ bags of rubbish. ______
5 When they eat lunch ~~Sunita~~ tells the others about the ring. ______
6 Lily can put a note about the ~~rubbish~~ in her building. ______

## 18 Language in the story

▶ SB, pp. 116–117

**Complete the sentences. Use words from the box.**

| about (2x) • at • for • of • over |
|---|

1 There's a big group in front ______ the youth centre.
2 Mr Davies is angry ______ the noise.
3 "Let's put good things ______ there," says Olga.
4 "Let's meet here ______ 12 o'clock for lunch," says Olga.
5 Buddy digs in the ground ______ a long time.
6 Lily tells the others ______ the Swap Place garage.

I can understand a story about green activities.

## 19 Words in Unit 4

**Write the words in the right list.**

~~chips~~ • ~~cloudy~~ • cold • on an estate • everywhere • friendly • in Germany • hot • ice cream • inside • loud • married • a meal • over there • rainy • quiet • snowy • sunny • in town • water

| How people are | Weather words | Where? | What you can eat or drink |
|---|---|---|---|
| ______ | *cloudy* ______ | ______ | *chips* ______ |
| ______ | ______ | ______ | ______ |
| ______ | ______ | ______ | ______ |
| ______ | ______ | ______ | ______ |
| | ______ | ______ | |
| | ______ | ______ | |

## 20 *e* or *y*?

a) Complete each verb with ***e*** or ***y***.

1 c l o s ___ 
2 ___ x p l a i n 
3 b u ___ 
4 c l ___ a n 
5 s t a ___ 
8 t r a v ___ l 
7 s ___ l l 
8 m ___ a n

b) Now write the right verb in each sentence.

1 The car is dirty. Can you ______________ it, please? – No, sorry, I can't. I'm busy.

2 Excuse me, does this shop ______________ clothes? – Yes, it does.

3 When does the ice rink ______________ ? – At 5.30 p.m.

4 I don't understand this sentence. Can you please ______________ it to me? – OK, of course.

5 Can you go to the market and ______________ some apples? – OK, how many do you want?

6 Do you often ______________ by train? – No, I don't.

7 It's late. Do you want to ______________ here? – Oh, thank you.

8 "Expensive" is a new word. I don't know it. What does it ______________ ? – Doesn't cost a lot.

## 21 Ask what something is like

**Fill the gaps with words from the boxes.**

| the new cinema • ~~your estate~~ • the noise • your neighbours • the weather |
|---|

| really boring • very expensive • really loud • sunny • unfriendly |
|---|

1 What's *your estate* ______ like? – It's ______.

2 What's ______ like? – It's ______.

3 What's ______ like? – It's ______.

4 What's ______ like? – It's ______.

5 What are ______ like? – They're ______.

## 22 Useful phrases for a short talk

**Find the words. Then complete the sentences.**

1 AUOBT My presentation is ______ my town.

2 TIHS In ______ photo you can see a busy shop in my town.

3 LTES' ______ look at this photo of my favourite cafe.

4 NAY Do you have ______ questions?

5 LINETSING Thank you for ______.

## 23 Listening and Speaking Speak English well

> Can you hear it? In *yes/no*-questions, the intonation goes up at the end of the sentence.

21
**a) Listen to these *yes/no*-questions.**

1 Do you like cooking?

2 Is it sunny today?

3 Does your town have a swimming pool?

4 Do you often eat chips?

5 Do you sometimes do new sports?

22
**b) Listen and repeat the questions.**

**c) Say the questions in a). Your partner answers. Then swap roles.**

*Do you like cooking?* *Yes, I do.* *No, I don't.*

### Three favourite words:

______________________

______________________

______________________

### Three difficult words:

______________________

______________________

______________________

### Three favourite phrases:

______________________

______________________

______________________

### My favourite page in Unit 4:

______________________

### Why:

______________________

### I remember:

Places in town: ______________________

______________________

Weather words: ______________________

A negative sentence with *doesn't* or *don't*: ______________________

A question with *do* or *does*: ______________________

Five question words: *when?,* ______________________

Where things are: *behind,* ______________________

______________________

### I think English is:

☐ not hard ☐ quite hard ☐ very hard

This is quite difficult:

☐ writing words ☐ saying words

☐ learning words ☐ using verbs

*What can you do?*
*You can practise more.*
*You can ask the teacher*
*or a friend for help.*

## 1 Word puzzles

a) **Write the places in the puzzle.**

1 You can watch films here.
2 Kids can do skateboarding here.
3 A place for sport on ice. (two words)
4 A (very) small park, often behind a house.
5 You can play or sit in the sun here, next to the sea.
6 A place with a lot of books and computers.
7 A building, or part of a building, where you can buy things like clothes.
8 This place has activities for teenagers. (two words)
9 A place in the centre of town where you can buy food and sometimes other things.
10 A place for people when they are really not well.

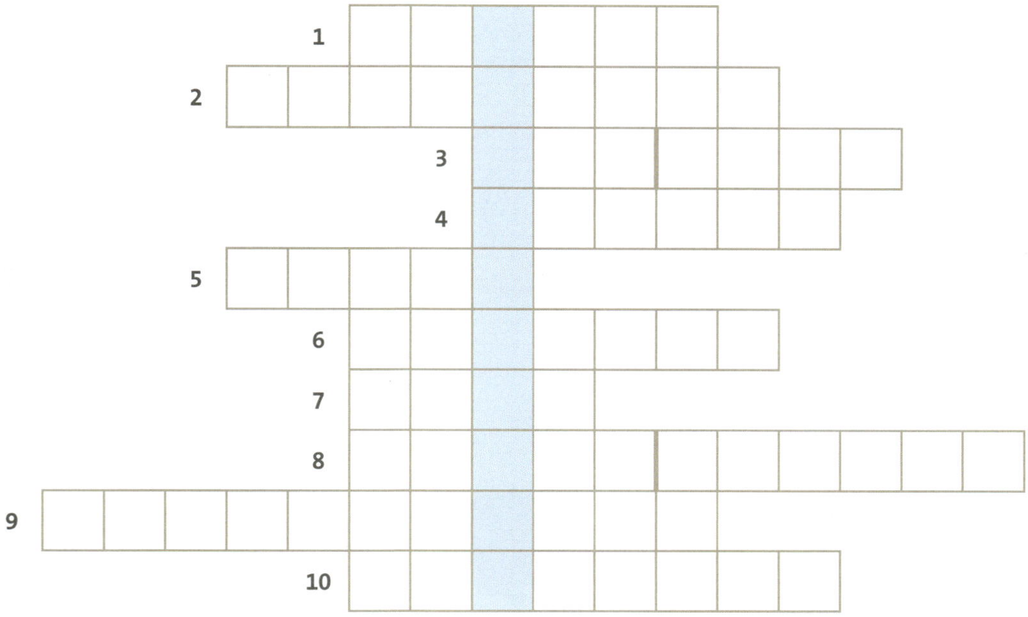


b) **What does the word in blue mean? Tick (✓) the correct sentence.**

1 The people who live next to you. ☐
2 The town or village where you live. ☐
3 The part of the town or village where you live. ☐

► Check

## 2 A great place near you

**Look again at the brochure about Thorpe Park on page 64 in exercise 15.**
**Then choose a great place near you and make a brochure for it.**
**Use some of the language in the text and brochure in exercise 15, for example:**

A fantastic fun park / swimming pool / skatepark / zoo / park / ... near ...
A place where all the family can have fun.
A day ticket isn't expensive.
Visitors can ...

# Unit 5
# Enjoy!

## 1 Lots of food

▸ SB, p. 135

**Look at the photos. Write the right word from the box under each photo.**

| bread • cake • cheese • cream • fruit • meat • peas • rice • spices • strawberries |
|---|

A

______

B

______

C
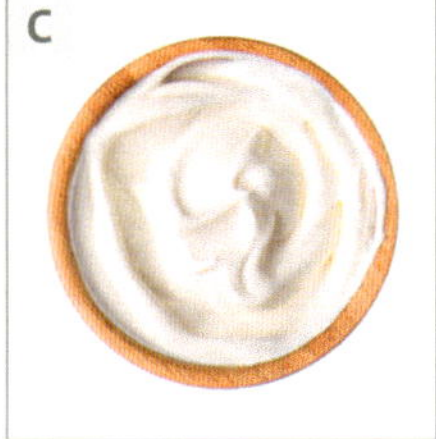
______

D

______

E

______

F

______

G

______

H

______

I

______

J

______

23

## 2 LISTENING Lunch at school

▸ SB, p. 135

**Oscar isn't happy. Listen and circle the right word..**

Mum usually gives me a (1) cheese / big sandwich for lunch on school days.

She always puts (2) water / fruit in my bag too because it's healthy.

But I don't want that! I want to have (3) pizza / a burger in the school

canteen like my friends – with (4) cola / chips!

And I want to have (5) chocolate / sweets too! It isn't fair!

> Be ready. Read the text before you listen.

I can talk about food.

## 3 The months of the year

▶ SB p.136

a) Write the missing letters in the months.

| | | | |
|---|---|---|---|
| Janua__y | __pril | July | Oc__ober |
| February | Ma__ | Augu__t | Novembe__ |
| Ma__ch | Jun__ | September | Decem__er |

b) Use your letters in 3a) to complete this word.

For my birthday I like:

_ _ _ _ w _ _ _ _ _ cake

## 4 Dates

▶ SB p.137

Write the dates in the right order.

the fifth of May • the tenth of January • the sixth of March • ~~the ninth of January~~ • the first of October • the eighth of May • the second of March • the seventh of June • the second of May • the third of June

1 *the ninth of January*
2 ______
3 ______
4 ______
5 ______
6 ______
7 ______
8 ______
9 ______
10 ______

## 5 A dialogue about a birthday party

▶ SB p.137

Write the questions in the dialogue.

1 Kyla's birthday party / is / when / ?

______ It's on Saturday 5th October.

2 does / what time / start / the party / ?

______ It's at 3 p.m.

3 the / is / party / where / ?

______ At her house.

4 activities / there / are / what / ?

______ Party games and dancing.

## 6 Party invitations

► SB, p. 137

When is (___)'s party?
What time does the party start?
Where is the party?
What activities are there?

Partner B: Look at page 87.
Partner A:
Ask partner B about parties 1 and 3. Write the answers.
Answer partner B's questions about parties 2 and 4.

**1 COME TO AMBER'S BIRTHDAY PARTY!**

When? ______
What time? ______
Where? ______
What? ______

**2 COME TO BEN'S SUMMER PARTY!**

When? Sunday 7th July
What time? At 12 o'clock
Where? At the beach
What? A barbecue

**3 COME TO MOLLY AND ANNA'S PARTY!**

When? ______
What time? ______
Where? ______
What? ______

**4 COME TO HAMID'S BIRTHDAY PARTY!**

When? Monday 2nd January
What time? At 2.30 p.m.
Where? At the sports centre
What? Trampolining

## 7 LISTENING Can you come to my party?

24

► SB, p. 137

a) Listen to six people. Can they come to Ben's party? Write (✓) or (✗).

b) Listen again and look at the pictures (A–F). Write the letters in the boxes.

1 Molly ____ ☐ 2 Hamid ____ ☐ 3 Chang ____ ☐
4 Anna ____ ☐ 5 Amber ____ ☐ 6 Uncle Tim ____ ☐

A

B

C

D

E

F

Erklär-film

## 8 LANGUAGE Present progressive Oscar's message to Ling

▶ SB, p. 139

Complete the message with: *'m / is / 's / are / 're.*

! (name) + is -> he / she + 's
(names) + are -> they + 're

*Hi Ling*

*Mum and dad ________ (1) sitting in the living room at the moment. They ________ (2) watching a really stupid film. They think I ________ (3) doing my homework, but I ________ (4) playing on my computer (shhhh!). Freddie ________ (5) staying with his friend and Olivia isn't here – she ________ (6) playing at a friend's house – so it's quiet ;-). What ________ (7) you doing?*

## 9 LANGUAGE Present progressive Who is doing what?

▶ SB, p. 139

Write sentences. Use the present progressive (*-ing* form).

! take -> taking • have -> having • sit -> sitting

1 *Amber is* ________
2 *Anna is* ________
3 *Hamid* ________
4 *Ben* ________
5 *Molly* ________

| | |
|---|---|
| Amber | have a shower |
| Anna | make lunch |
| Hamid | juggle |
| Ben | text her friend |
| Molly | sleep on the sofa |

## 10 LANGUAGE Present progressive What is the girl doing?

▶ SB, p. 139

a) Look at the pictures. Write what you think the girl is doing.

brush her teeth • clean her room • eat something • listen to music • play the guitar • take a photo

1 
2 
3 
4 
5 
6 

1 *She's playing* ________
2 *She's* ________
3 ________
4 ________
5 ________
6 ________

b) Mime an action. Your partner guesses what it is.

*I think you're eating an orange.*

## 11 Language Present progressive It's Saturday afternoon

► SB, p. 139

a) Ling's mum isn't at home. There's a note for Ling – but when her mum phones, Ling *isn't* doing what her mum wants. Write what Ling *isn't* doing.

*Ling – please do these things:*
*– tidy your room*
*– brush the cat*
*– do your homework*
*– buy fruit at the shop*
*– clean the toilet*
*Mum xx*

1 *Ling isn't tidying* her room.
2 *She* ________ the cat.
3 ________ her homework.
4 ________ fruit at the shop.
5 ________ the toilet.

b) Ling's mum phones. Complete Ling's answer.

! plan → planning

*Ling, are you doing the things in my note?*

*Oh, OK – great idea!*

*Sorry, Mum. I* *'m not* ________ *(1 not do) those things, and I* ________ *(2 not look) at your note! I* ________ *(3 make) a birthday cake for grandma and I* ________ *(4 plan) a party!*

## 12 Language Present progressive What is happening in the photos?

► SB, p. 139

a) Ling is showing Oscar photos from her grandma's party. Complete the sentences.

Look at these photos, Oscar. In this photo, we ________ (1 play) a game. Well, my brother ________ (2 not play) – he ________ (3 take) the photo! And here, my parents ________ (4 dance) together. But they ________ (5 not dance) very well! They're so funny!

– What ________ you ________ (6 do) in this photo, Ling?

– I ________ (7 sing) karaoke, but the others ________ (8 not listen). Maybe because I ________ (9 not sing) very well!

b) Now check your answers in 12a).
1 Are there always two parts to the verb: 'm / 'm not / 's / isn't / 're / aren't + verb + -ing?
2 Does the second part end in -ing?



I can talk about birthdays and parties

## 13 A birthday present

▸ SB, p. 140

Ling, Oscar and Hamid are talking about Amber's birthday.
Write the right words from the box.

already • idea • let's • maybe • perfect • present • sure

**Ling** Let's buy a ______________ for Amber. It's her party soon.

**Hamid** That's a good ______________, Ling. I know! ______________ buy a sweatshirt for her!

**Oscar** Mmm ... I'm not ______________ – they're quite expensive.

**Ling** And Amber ______________ has lots of sweatshirts. ______________ a smart hat?

**Hamid** That's ______________! Let's look online.

## 14 A thank you email

▸ SB, p. 140

a) READING Read Amber's thank you email and look at the pictures.
Tick (✓) the presents from her grandparents.

to grandparents55@example.com
from contactamber@example.com

Dear Grandma and Grandpa
Thank you very much for the money and the juggling balls. I really like them. They're a great present because I love circuses and I'm learning to do circus tricks.
Amber xx

A  ☐

B  ☐

C  ☐

D  ☐

b) WRITING Now write Amber's email to Uncle Matt.

*presents*: music books *Amber loves*: music
*she's learning to*: play the guitar

Dear ...
Thank you very much for the ... I really like them.
They're a great present because I love ...
and I'm learning to ...

to Matty123@example.com
from contactamber@example.com

______________________________________________

______________________________________________

______________________________________________

______________________________________________

## 15 LANGUAGE *much, many* Things for a party

► SB, p. 141

Erklär-film

a) Look at the food and drinks. Write *S* if they are singular, *P* if they are plural.

b) Then complete the questions with *how much* or *how many*.

A

bread ☐

B

carrots ☐

E

sausages ☐

F

cheese ☐

C

ham ☐

D

cola ☐

G

strawberries ☐

H

lemonade ☐

1 ____________ bread do we have?

2 ____________ carrots do we have?

3 ____________ ham do we have?

4 ____________ cola do we have?

5 ____________ sausages do we have?

6 ____________ cheese do we have?

7 ____________ strawberries do we have?

8 ____________ lemonade do we have?

## 16 LANGUAGE *much, many* Amber's party

► SB, p. 141

a) Uncle Matt asks Amber about her party. Circle the correct words.

**Uncle** How many / much people are coming to your party, Amber?

**Amber** Oh, it's a big party – a lot of friends are coming.

**Uncle** How many / much time do you have before the party?

**Amber** Not many / much – it's at 7.30. And there are a lot of things to do! The hall at the youth centre must look nice – but we don't have many / much balloons. And we don't have many / much cola.

**Uncle** It's OK, I can go to the shops. How many / much things do you need?

**Amber** Oh thanks, Uncle Matt! Mum can make a shopping list for you.

!

In verneinten Sätzen und Fragen verwendest du
– *many* bei Dingen, die du zählen kannst (viele),
– *much* bei Dingen, die du nicht zählen kannst (viel).

I can talk about party food and activities

## 17 Ling is making a carrot cake

▶ SB, p. 144

a) Look at the pictures and write the correct words from the list.

Carrot cake

230 g grated[1] carrot
2 eggs
120 ml oil
160 g brown sugar
1 teaspoon vanilla
230 g flour
1 teaspoon baking powder
1 teaspoon cinnamon[2]
¼ teaspoon salt

100 g icing sugar
50 g butter
200 g cream cheese[3]

1

______

2

______

3

______

4

______

5

______

6

______

b) Complete the sentences. Write the verbs in the ing-form.

| | | Picture |
|---|---|---|
| 1 | Ling is *adding* (add) the eggs. | B |
| 2 | Ling is ______ (mix) the eggs with the carrot, oil, sugar and vanilla. | |
| 3 | She's ______ (add) the flour, baking powder, salt and cinnamon. | |
| 4 | She's ______ (put) the mixture into the oven (190° for 50–60 minutes). | |
| 5 | She's ______ (make) the icing with icing sugar, butter and cream cheese. | |
| 6 | She's ______ (put) the icing on the cake. | |

c) Match the pictures A–F with the sentences 1–6 in b). Write the letters in the boxes.

A

B

C

D

E

F
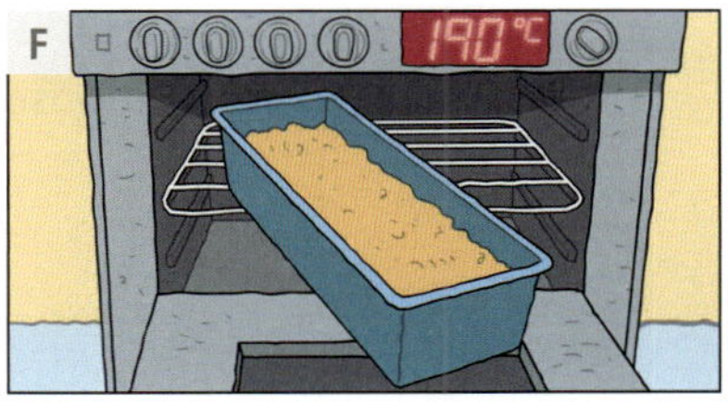


[1] **grated** *gerieben* [2] **cinnamon** *Zimt* [3] **cream cheese** *Frischkäse (Doppelrahm stufe)*

## 18 MEDIATION My favourite dish

▸ SB, p. 145

**Your friend finds this post on a website: My favourite dish. She asks you questions about it. Answer her questions.**

**Harry**

*Hi everybody! My favourite dish is a chocolate dessert that my grandma makes. It's a special dish for me because grandma always makes it for my birthday. She makes it with egg, not much flour, cream, cocoa, sugar and a lot of chocolate. And she puts strawberries on top of it. Yum - it's delicious! But she also makes a fruit salad for my brother Andy because he's allergic to chocolate.* ✓

1 Warum ist diese Nachspeise etwas Besonderes für Harry?

________________________________

2 Woraus besteht die Nachspeise?

________________________________

3 Für wen macht sie eine andere Nachspeise und warum?

________________________________

## 19 What is in your favourite dish?

▸ SB, p. 145

a) LISTENING **Listen to three people. Tick (✓) four things in each person's favourite dish.**

25

| 1 Hazel – a British dish | 2 Erin – Irish stew | 3 Marta – vegetarian risotto |
|---|---|---|
| ☐ chips | ☐ meat | ☐ rice |
| ☐ carrots | ☐ ham | ☐ cheese |
| ☐ peas | ☐ rice | ☐ tomatoes |
| ☐ tomato sauce | ☐ vegetables | ☐ cheese sauce |
| ☑ fish | ☐ carrots | ☐ potatoes |
| ☐ curry sauce | ☐ spices | ☐ curry powder |

b) **You can eat one of the dishes in exercises 18 and 19a). Which dish do you choose and why?**

I choose ____________________ 's dish

because I like ____________________

and I don't like ____________________ .

*Mmmm, yum!*

I can describe my favourite dish ✓

## 20 VIEWING Watch and learn

► SB, p. 149

**Watching the video can help you understand new words. Tick (✓) and write the correct answers.**

**Part 1 (00:37 to 01:09)** *Watch* Emir when he says "**A hundred percent**[1]" **(100%)**

What does he mean? A ☐ Yes, I *really* want to come. B ☐ Hmm ... Maybe ...

**Parts 5 & 6 (04:17 to 05:31)** Watch what they buy. Write the German words:

**candles** = ____________________ **napkins** = ____________________

## 21 VIEWING You can act

► SB, p. 149

a) **Watch Part 2 (01:10 to 02:10) again and read the script. Listen to *how* they say the sentences.**

**Daisy** Is that for Gloria?

**Emir** Yes.

**Daisy** Here. A list – for tomorrow.

**Emir** Birthday cake, candles, balloons, ... and how about[2] a birthday dare?

**Daisy** Hmm ... A birthday dare? Yes. Why not? Give me a pen. Quick! And that's for you ...

**Emir** You are sooo bad!

**Daisy** So ... let's do it?

b) **Practise saying the sentences with a partner. Partner A is Daisy, partner B is Emir.**

c) **Now play the video with no sound. You and your partner say the words for Daisy and Emir. Do it lots of times so you're really good.**

You can watch again and copy *how* Daisy and Emir say the sentences.

## 22 VIEWING Daisy's imaginary[3] friend

► SB, p. 149

**Watch Part 3 (02:11 to 03:06). Listen to what Daisy says to her imaginary friend, Sota. What do you think Sota says to her? Tick (✓) the correct answer.**

1 a) ☐ Please. b) ☐ Thanks.

2 a) ☐ I'm good. Are you? b) ☐ I'm tired after the journey.

3 a) ☐ When is the party? b) ☐ Where is the party?

4 a) ☐ But I don't know Gloria. b) ☐ But I don't have a present for Gloria.

[1] **percent** *Prozent* [2] **how about ...? = what about ...?** [3] **imaginary** *Fantasie-, vorgestellt*

## 23 When is it?

Write the dates in words.

1 05/05 *the ____ of ____*
2 08/07 ____________
3 01/12 ____________
4 03/06 ____________
5 10/03 ____________
6 02/01 ____________

eighth • fifth • first • second • tenth • third

December • January • July • June • March • May

## 24 It's a kind of…

a) The letters *a, e, i, o, u* are missing in these words. Write the words correctly – in the right groups.

b-n-n- c-rr-t ch-ck-n c-ff-- h-m l-m-n m-l-n

l-m-n-d- p-- p-t-t- s--s-g- str-wb-rry t-- w-t-r

| It's a kind of fruit | It's a kind of meat | It's a kind of drink | It's a kind of vegetable |
|---|---|---|---|
| | | | |
| | | | |
| | | | |
| | | | |

b) Write at least five more food words – things that aren't fruit, meat, drinks or vegetables!

▸ Digital help

________________________________________

## 25 Listening Ling's food quiz

26 a) Ling is describing food. Listen and circle the six right words in the bowl.

27 b) Listen and check your answers.

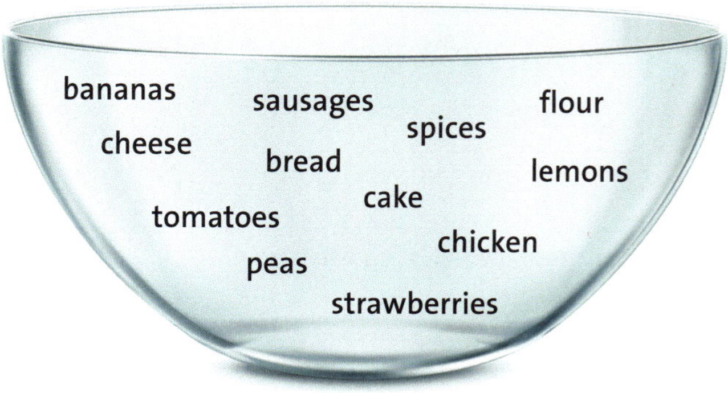

## 26 What do you do?

**Complete the sentences with the correct verbs from the box.**

cut • enjoy • fry • guess • put • sleep • wear

1 You ____________ clothes.

2 You ____________ an answer (if you don't know it).

3 You ____________ a happy afternoon with friends.

4 When you're tired, you go to bed and ____________.

5 When you make a cake, you ____________ it in the oven.

6 To make chips, you ____________ the potatoes before you ____________ them.

## 27 Words in Unit 5

a) **Match words 1-6 with their meanings. Draw lines and write the right letters in the boxes below.**

| | |
|---|---|
| 1 invitation | **W** things that are not the same |
| 2 juggle | **R** really, really good |
| 3 differences | **O** play with two or three balls at the same moment |
| 4 amazing | **D** lots of people like it |
| 5 recipe | **P** this asks you to come to a party |
| 6 popular | **E** this tells you how to make a cake or a dish |

| 1 | P | 2 | | 3 | | 4 | | 5 | | 6 | |
|---|---|---|---|---|---|---|---|---|---|---|---|

b) **Complete the sentence with your answers letters in a).**

When you make hot chocolate, you use cocoa ________ and sugar.

## 28 Listening and Speaking Speak English well

28

a) **How do you say the s at the end of the word? Listen to the words and sentences and write s or z.**

potatoes – ___ strawberries – ___ carrots – ___ melons – ___

lemons – ___ peas – ___ cakes – ___

bananas – ___ salads – ___ desserts – ___ packets – ___

*After the sounds **p**, **t**, **c/k** and **th**, you say **s**.*

b) **Listen again and repeat the words.**

**Three favourite words:**

____________________

____________________

____________________

| Three difficult words: | to write | to say |
|---|---|---|
| ____________ | ☐ | ☐ |
| ____________ | ☐ | ☐ |
| ____________ | ☐ | ☐ |

## I remember:

Twelve months: ____________________

Some things to eat and drink: ____________________

Some party things: ____________________

How to talk about buying birthday presents: **Complete these sentences.**

Let's *b*________ a present for Ling. What *a*________ a T-shirt? Why *d*________ we buy a book?

How to say what someone is / isn't doing: **Write three sentences.**

Scout – sing / dance / not fly

*Scout* ____________________

*She* ____________________

____________________

## English and me:

| For me: | easy | sometimes hard | hard |
|---|---|---|---|
| listening exercises are ... | | | |
| reading exercises are ... | | | |
| writing words is ... | | | |
| saying words is ... | | | |
| learning words is ... | | | |
| using verbs is ... | | | |

*Ask a friend to test you on the words in your VOCAB FILE. Practise the difficult words. That helps with listening, reading and writing!*

## 1 Word snake puzzle

**Find the missing words in the word snake and complete the sentences.**

1 Noah's birthday party is a ____________ party.
2 I love doing magic ____________ !
3 July is a ____________ in summer.
4 The eleventh month: ____________
5 I'm tired. I want to ____________ .
6 Phone or ____________ if you can come to my party.
7 3rd: ____________
8 The colour of custard: ____________

EEPCIRCUSTXTTRICKSTEHMONTH NOVEMBERLOWSLEEPRDTEXTYWOTHIRDCRIYELLOWCK

## 2 Can you find the differences?

**Find the differences and write what they are.**

Six differences - good!
Eight differences - great!

the girl is ...ing
it's ...

| In picture A ... | But in picture B ... |
| --- | --- |
| the people are ____________ | they're ____________ |
| ____________ | ____________ |
| ____________ | ____________ |
| ____________ | ____________ |
| ____________ | ____________ |
| ____________ | ____________ |
| ____________ | ____________ |
| ____________ | ____________ |

► Check

## 1 Tia's house

Write the names of the rooms.

bathroom • bedroom • kitchen • living room • office • toilet

______

______

______

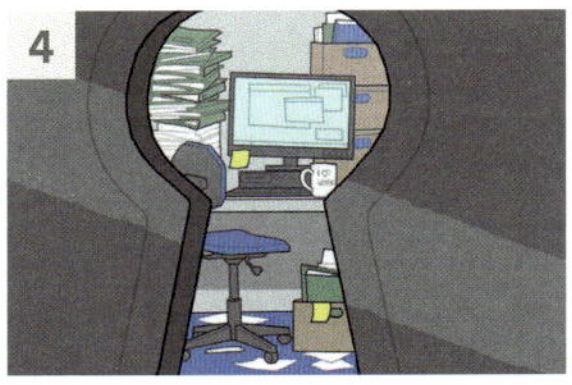


______

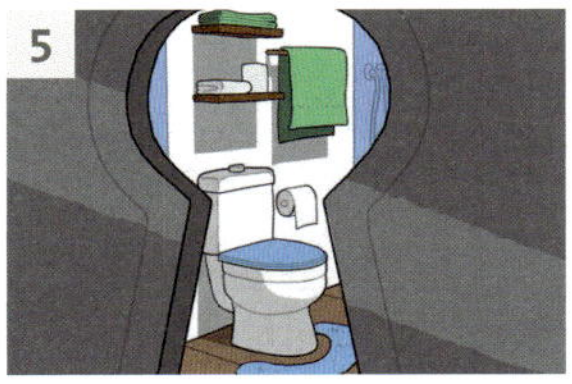


______

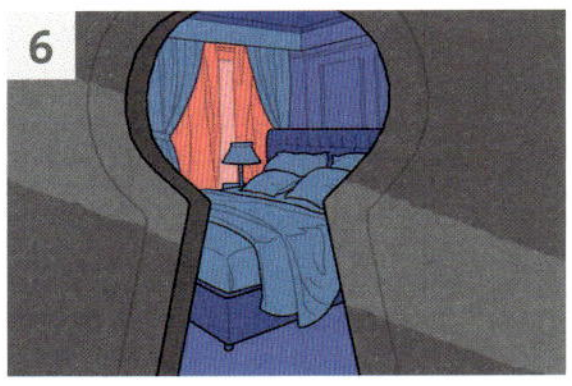


______

## 2 Tia's family

Circle the right word.

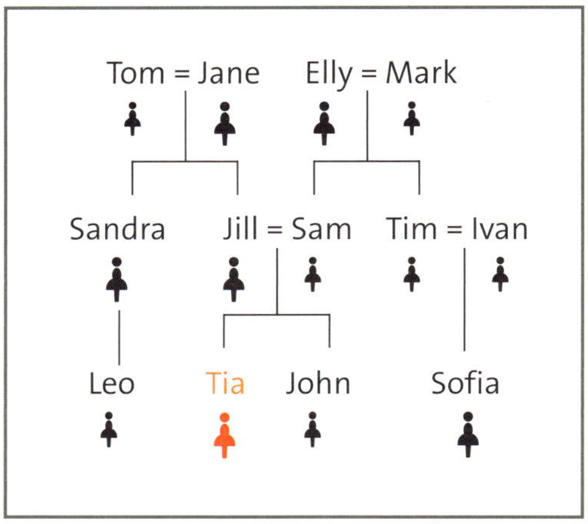


1 John is Tia's brother / cousin.
2 Jill is Tia's grandma / mum.
3 Elly is Tia's aunt / grandma.
4 Tia is Leo's cousin / aunt.
5 Tim is Tia's uncle / cousin.
6 Sandra is Tia's aunt / sister.
7 Sandra is Jill's sister / cousin.

## 3 Tia talks about her family

Write the correct words: *my / your / his / her / our / their*.

*Tom is my grandpa and Jane is ______ grandma. They live near here, at ______ daughter Sandra's house. Aunt Sandra is really nice. ______ boy, Leo, comes here on Saturdays. He often brings ______ friend, Ali, and we all go on ______ bikes. What about you? Tell me about ______ family.*

► Check

Erklär-film

## 4 Tia talks to her friend Oscar

▸ Digital help

Circle the right form of the simple present.

**Tia** Are you always busy at the weekend, Oscar?

**Oscar** Yes, I am. I go / goes to football training every Saturday morning. My sister like / likes the park, so we play / plays games there together in the afternoon. My parents don't come / doesn't come because they're too busy. Do / Does you often go to the park, Tia?

**Tia** Well, I don't go / doesn't go there very often. But uncle Tim take / takes me and my cousin to the swimming pool every Sunday. He don't like / doesn't like swimming, so he have / has a drink in the cafe. Where do / does you go on Sunday, Oscar?

**Oscar** Mum and I sometimes visit / visits my grandma, but we don't see / doesn't see her every Sunday. She always give / gives me chocolate!

## 5 Tia and her friends talk about where they live

**Match the beginnings and ends of the sentences. Write A-G in the boxes below.**

| | | |
|---|---|---|
| 1 The streets near my house are often dirty ... | ☐ | A so I think they aren't very friendly. |
| 2 There isn't much noise in our street, ... | ☐ | B they sell ice cream and things like that. |
| 3 Lots of people go to the shopping centre, ... | ☐ | C so it's nice and quiet here. |
| 4 The people here never talk to me, ... | ☐ | D so our estate is nice and clean. |
| 5 We have no rubbish in the streets, ... | ☐ | E with rubbish in them. |
| 6 There's a shop where ... | ☐ | F lots of interesting activities there. |
| 7 Our youth centre is great because there are ... | ☐ | G so it's always busy there. |

▸ Check

## Unit 4 Topic 2 | Exercise 12

► WB, p. 62 ► SB, p. 112

Partner B: You want to know:
Is York a good place for a holiday in England?

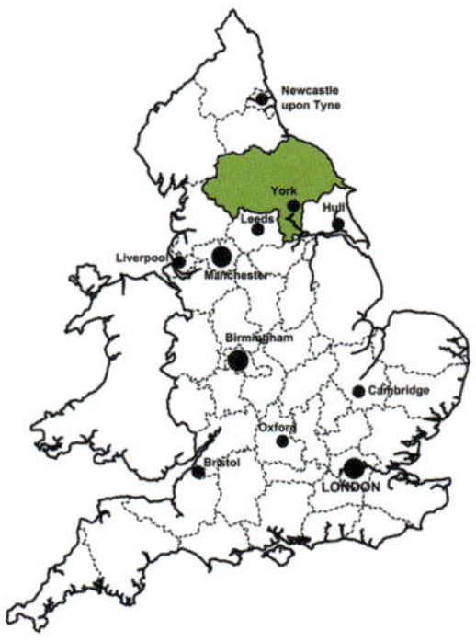


a) Write the questions about York. Put the words in the right order.

1 York / a train museum / does / have / ?

Does York have ______________________ ☐

2 a marina / does / or beach / have / York / ?

______________________ ☐

3 have / nice old buildings / does / York / ?

______________________ ☐

4 a big / York / football stadium / have / does / ?

______________________ ☐

5 shops / does / have / York / interesting / ?

______________________ ☐

b) Your partner wants to know about Devon. Look at the information.

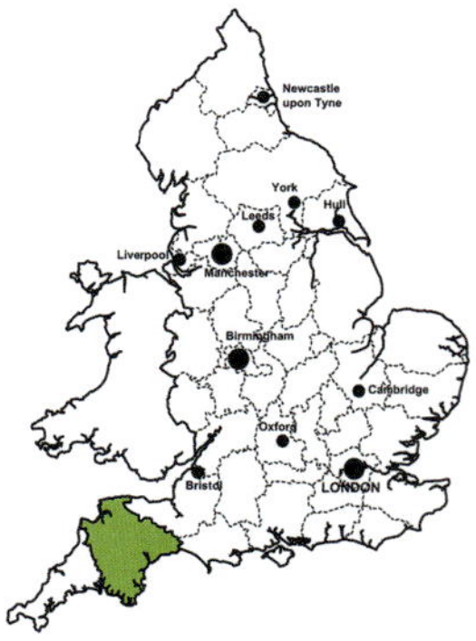


Devon has great beaches and is great for windsurfing. It also has lots of good places for walking. But Devon doesn't have good football clubs and doesn't have many big cities.

c) Your partner asks you about Devon.
Answer your partner's questions. Use short answers: *Yes, it does. / No, it doesn't.*

d) Now ask your questions about York. Put a tick (✓) in the box for yes, an (✕) for no.

e) Check your answers with your partner.

## Unit 5 Topic 1 | Exercise 6

▶ WB, p. 72 ▶ SB, p. 137

Partner B:
Answer partner A's questions about parties 1 and 3.
Ask partner A about parties 2 and 4 and write the answers.

When is (___)'s party?
What time does it start?
Where is the party?
What activities are there?

**1**

**COME TO AMBER'S BIRTHDAY PARTY!**

When? Saturday 4th June

What time? At 7.30 p.m.

Where? At the youth centre

What? Dancing

**2**

**COME TO BEN'S SUMMER PARTY!**

When? ______________________

What time? ______________________

Where? ______________________

What? ______________________

**3**

**COME TO MOLLY AND ANNA'S PARTY!**

When? Friday 1st March

What time? At 7 p.m.

Where? At Anna's house

What? Great party games

**4**

**COME TO HAMID'S BIRTHDAY PARTY!**

When? ______________________

What time? ______________________

Where? ______________________

What? ______________________

| Typical tasks | Häufige Arbeitsanweisungen |
|---|---|
| Act the conversation / part. | Führt das Gespräch / die Szene vor. |
| Answer the questions / partner B's questions. | Beantworte die Fragen / Partner/in Bs Fragen. |
| Ask questions. | Stelle Fragen. |
| Check with your partner. | Überprüfe mit deiner Partnerin / deinem Partner. |
| Choose the correct verbs / a person / ... | Wähle die richtigen Verben / eine Person / ... |
| Circle the right word / correct verb / ... | Kreise das richtige Wort / das richtige Verb / ... ein. |
| Complete the questions / message / ... | Vervollständige die Fragen / die Nachricht / ... |
| Cross out the numbers / wrong things / ... | Streiche die Nummern / die falschen Dinge / ... durch. |
| Draw pictures / lines / ... | Zeichne / Male Bilder / Linien / ... |
| Fill the gaps with the right words. | Vervollständige die Lücken mit den richtigen Wörtern. |
| Find the answers / right picture / ... | Finde die Antworten / das richtige Bild / ... |
| Highlight the letters / words / ... | Markiere die Buchstaben / Wörter / ... |
| Listen again. | Höre nochmal zu. |
| Listen and check / read / write / ... | Höre zu und überprüfe / lies / schreibe / ... |
| Listen to the words / sentences / people / ... | Höre dir die Wörter / Sätze / Leute / ... an. |
| Look at the picture / answers / ... | Schau dir das Bild / die Antwort / ... an. |
| Match the pictures / ... with the sentences / ... | Ordne die Bilder / ... den Sätzen / ... zu. |
| Practise with a partner. | Übe mit einem/r Partner/in. |
| Put a cross in the box for the wrong sentences. | Setze ein Kreuzchen ins Kästchen für die falschen Sätze. |
| Put a tick in the box for the correct sentences / in the right boxes. | Setze ein Häkchen ins Kästchen für die richtigen Sätze / in die richtigen Kästchen. |
| Put the words in the right order. | Setze die Wörter in die richtige Reihenfolge. |
| Read about ... | Lies über ... |
| Read the messages / sentences / text / ... | Lies die Nachrichten / Sätze / den Text / ... |
| Right (✓) or wrong (✗)? / True (T) or false (F)? | Richtig oder falsch? |
| Swap roles. | Wechselt die Rollen. |
| Talk to a partner. | Sprich mit einem/r Partner/in. |
| Tick the correct definition / the hobbies / ... | Hake alle richtigen Definitionen / Hobbys / ... ab. |
| Underline ... | Unterstreiche ... |
| Use the answers / letters / ... in the box. | Benutze die Antworten / Buchstaben / ... aus dem Kasten. |
| Use words from the box. | Benutze die Wörter aus dem Kasten. |
| Watch part 1/2/... (again). | Sieh dir Teil 1/2/... (nochmal) an. |
| Write about six sports / your grandma / ... | Schreibe über sechs Sportarten / deine Oma / ... |
| Write definitions / the answers / the sentences / ... | Schreibe die Definitionen / die Antworten / die Sätze / ... |